KEEP WHAT YOU OWN

KEEP

WHAT

PROTECT YOUR

MONEY, PROPERTY,

AND FAMILY FROM

COURTS, CREDITORS,

AND THE IRS

YOU

OWN

ADAM STARCHILD

PALADIN PRESS
BOULDER, COLORADO

Also by Adam Starchild:

Protect Your Assets: How to Avoid Falling
Victim to the Government's Forfeiture Laws

Reviving the American Dream:
Stop "Just Getting By" and Build Real
Wealth

Swiss Money Secrets: How You Can Legally
Hide Your Money in Switzerland

Using Offshore Havens for Privacy and Profits

Keep What You Own: Protect Your Money, Property,
and Family from Courts, Creditors, and the IRS
by Adam Starchild

Copyright © 1995 by Adam Starchild
ISBN 0-87364-834-X
Printed in the United States of America

Published by Paladin Press, a division of
Paladin Enterprises, Inc., P.O. Box 1307,
Boulder, Colorado 80306, USA.
(303) 443-7250

Direct inquiries and/or orders to the above address.

PALADIN, PALADIN PRESS, and the "horse head" design
are trademarks belonging to Paladin Enterprises and
registered in United States Patent and Trademark Office.

ontents

Introduction 1

Chapter 1
Only Comprehensive Planning Will Succeed 9

Chapter 2
Avoiding the Fraudulent Conveyance Trap 17

Chapter 3
False Asset Protection in Joint Ownership 23

Chapter 4
Traditional Judgment-Proofing Techniques 27

Chapter 5
Using Corporations to Limit Liability 33

Chapter 6
Using a Secret Foreign Corporation. 53

Chapter 7
The Limited Liability Company 63

Chapter 8
Limited Partnerships: An Authentic Judgment-
Proofing Device 71

Chapter 9
Legal Insurance: It Does Exist 93

Chapter 10
The Trust as Asset Protector 95

Chapter 11
The Swiss Annuity: Judgment-Proof and a
High Return 121

Chapter 12
The Advanced Strategies that Few Lawyers Know 145

Chapter 13
The High Ground of Judgment-Proofing 157

About the Author. 161

Introduction

IT CAN HAPPEN TO ANYONE

The purpose of this book is to alert that portion of the population of the United States that is not already aware of the risks posed to it from our legal system. In the past, it was the practice in this country that when a person wished to retain a lawyer to sue someone, he paid a lawyer a fee and the lawyer examined the issues and proceeded based on the merits of the case. This is no longer the case in America.

Due to the contingency system, we now have lawsuits being filed at the rate of 100 million cases a year. Many of these suits have nothing to do with right and wrong, but instead are predicated on the desire of one party to extract wealth from another party. In many cases, this equation is not predicated on the desire to extract real wealth, but instead to extract small payments as "nuisance" settlements because it is cheaper to pay than fight.

If this is not bad enough, another part of the problem is for those who are not being sued—the taxpayers who must maintain the court system's costs to handle this litigation.

If lawsuits continue at their current pace, it can be estimated that each wage earning person in this country (80 percent of the population) will be sued five times. One does not have to lose even one of these cases in order to lose his wealth; the cost of litigation alone can be onerous enough. Even if one is lucky enough to make it through life without becoming a target of the legal maze, at time of death, under today's law, the federal government will take roughly 50 percent of a family's wealth when transfers of money over $1.2 million are made from mother and father to children. Several bills have been proposed that call for even more oppressive taxation.

If you have attempted to pursue the American dream of wealth, independence, and the ability to control your life, you may be disappointed by these numbers. In fact, you may be frightened. For the first time in your life, you may be considering expatriation. (Every year, at least 250,000 people become expatriates of the United States.)

In this book I examine the issues that are causing these fears, provide some solutions, and direct you to little-known sources that can provide the kind of planning and support that is necessary in today's world.

I shall delve into some situations that have actually arisen for ordinary people as well as those who have acquired wealth and truly become unmoving targets in today's society, and I will examine the issues involved from both of these viewpoints.

For many people, the threshold issue in judgment-proofing is whether or not they need it. Many people believe that a lawsuit or asset forfeiture won't happen to them, because they don't do anything that is dangerous. The reality of life in America is that you don't have to do anything dangerous; all you really have to do is be in the wrong place at the wrong time. Ordinary people have extraordinary problems. In many cases these problems are not problems of their own doing but simply matters of circumstance.

Imagine a group of business partners getting together for an informal lunch to discuss their work. A partner asks one of the secretaries in the office to take one of the partners' cars and go to a local restaurant to pick up their lunch order. Unbeknownst to the partners, the secretary has a poor driving record: several accidents and speeding tickets. The secretary leaves the building, climbs into a partner's car, and proceeds to pick up lunch. During this trip, the employee exceeds the speed limit and pays more attention to the radio than to an upcoming stop sign. She runs the stop sign, smashes into a car, and kills the other driver. One would think a subsequent lawsuit would simply blame the employee for her negligence, but unfortunately this is not the case.

What occurs at this point is the tragedy and trauma of American life. All of the partners are sued as a result of their negligence in not determining that this driver was in fact unsafe. More importantly, because the driver was on company business, the heirs of the deceased now seek retribution from the partners. The partners' homes, college funds, boats, vacation homes, even their business are up for grabs.

Several hundred thousand dollars is spent attempting to defend this suit. Unfortunately, the case is not settled because the main suing party, one of the remaining family, continues to expect more money to be found and more wealth to be uncovered. In many cases, one of the primary financial elements sought is insurance. In days gone by, insurance was a protector of the family and the business. Nowadays it often acts as a target.

•••

A father dies. He has built a substantial business. Remaining are two daughters who have never really participated in the business but feel that they are absolutely bound to step into it and manage it in order to protect

3

the family fortune. For many years, a distant cousin of the family has participated in the business in a management, but not a leadership, position. Upon taking over the business, the young daughters determine that this cousin has been less than trustworthy. He has stolen money from the company and mismanaged it, and now the company is in danger of going bankrupt. In order to save the precious assets that remain, the daughters decide to sell the company. They find a willing buyer and are able to consummate the transaction.

The cousin now files suit claiming that the father had promised him the business for his long and superior work. In the ensuing years, tens of thousands of dollars is spent on legal fees. The daughters attempt to protect their wealth as the cousin comes at them with various legal maneuvers. The question of right and wrong becomes convoluted. The cousin, attempting to extort settlement money from the daughters, threatens to turn them in to the Internal Revenue Service (IRS) and the Environmental Protection Agency (EPA). Even though there is no apparent violation of IRS or EPA regulations, such investigations can be expensive and time-consuming, and there is always the fear that some unknown and inadvertent violation will cause a forfeiture of their wealth. Numerous motions take place in the court case and each daughter is removed from and included in the lawsuit at different times.

Unfortunately, all of this takes time and money. And most unfortunately, it takes the daughters from their main business activities. Lawyers come and lawyers go, continually advising the sisters as to their next course of action. Money is spent but nothing ever seems to happen. One daughter has a particularly large amount of "liquid capital"—capital that is subject to a lien by a judgment creditor in the event she loses this case. She continually asks her lawyers what she can do to protect herself and their answer is to continue to litigate.

4

•••

In our society, drugs have become a tremendous evil. Many times law enforcement authorities need to be able to show progress in the war on drugs in order to secure their positions as elected officials. A bust goes down and a pharmacist is arrested for allegedly selling black-market drugs to dope fiends. Upon further examination, it turns out that the local law enforcement authorities had set up the pharmacist. They sent undercover police officers to his pharmacy seeking drugs through use of prescriptions for not only illegal drugs but drugs like penicillin that one would not associate with narcotics traffic. Our young pharmacist, who has not had the opportunity in his life to build up huge amounts of wealth, finds his business sold, his house in danger, and his retirement funds now unobtainable. He is as afraid of going to jail as he is of losing his wealth. If he goes to jail, his ability to provide financial support for his family will be tremendously curtailed. There must be steps that can be taken to protect the wealth of this individual.

•••

An elderly gentleman walks into a pharmacy and asks for a specific drug. While his prescription is being filled, he asks one of the office staff for a glass of water. The employee is distracted and accidentally serves the man the wrong glass, which has a tasteless and odorless drug mixed in it. The man drinks the liquid, has a heart attack, and dies. The employee responsible for this action is somewhat new and has had little training. However, this employee's purpose and job description are to operate a cash register and act as a cashier.

When suit is filed for several million dollars, the employee is not mentioned but the pharmacist is. The pharmacist realizes that there is no choice but to settle the case, resulting in wasted years of hard work when his accumulated assets go toward paying the settlement. He is lucky that this case did not go to trial, in which case far greater economic damage could have been done. Because his assets are vulnerable and his wealth is obtainable by the judgment creditor, he submits to the settlement in order to go on with his life without the burden of a judgment against future earnings as well.

•••

A woman is successful in her business selling real estate. In some years, she makes over $100,000. Her husband, a not-too-successful businessman, needs funding for his new business. He turns to his wife during this time and elicits support from her. She funds the business, it starts to do well, and money is made. The husband comes to his wife and confesses to an affair with another woman. The wife is shocked and disappointed. In a rage she leaves the family household in order to seek sanctuary with her parents. The husband takes the children and successfully sues for alimony and child support.

The wife begins a new business and becomes successful, and the husband's business begins to falter. He continues bringing action against her for more and more alimony and child support. Her new business venture suffers for obvious reasons. It simply is impossible to carry the burden of this court action and at the same time provide the time and energies that are necessary for her business. If there were only a way to protect her newfound business success from these creditors.

•••

A man who works for himself acquiring properties, managing them, and providing housing for many people, finds himself the subject of a lawsuit brought by what are known as "squatters": persons who enter property that is vacant, set up households, and live rent-free with no electricity, no water, and none of the creature comforts most of us require. These persons have small children who eat the paint coming off the walls in this property and suffer lead poisoning as a result. The squatting family now files suit against the homeowner, who must defend himself in court. How much more unfair can it be for someone to enter your property without your knowledge or permission, do damage to their children through their own negligence, and turn around and attempt to sue you?

•••

These are examples of ordinary people with extraordinary problems. The days are gone when only the rich and powerful are subject to lawsuits. The days are gone when right or wrong truly determines whether a suit is filed or dismissed. It is an unfortunate thing for individuals in the United States to conclude that their safety depends on the fairness of others, because this is not the case. It is imperative that families and businesses today understand that they are at risk, and that problems can ensue. In this book, I examine many traditional methods that don't work—such as putting assets in a spouse's name—and then show you the methods that do work and have been upheld by the courts.

1 Only Comprehensive Planning Will Succeed

There are several options that people are faced with in developing an asset protection plan. Some of them are good, some of them are not.

One of the unfortunate options that many people opt for is to lie and misrepresent. Let it be known, without any doubt, that plans of this nature simply will not work, for many reasons. First, telling untruths during a court action is obviously one that can have severe ramifications. People go to jail for perjury, fines are imposed, and careers are ruined. It is absolutely critical to judgment-proofing that people are compelled to tell the truth to the court and that they understand that only by telling the truth can they succeed.

Of equal importance is the issue of fraudulent conveyance, which I shall examine later. It is critical to understand that by being truthful and not making your plan vulnerable, you serve your business, your family, and all parties involved with a bulletproof arrangement.

It is also true that the protection a comprehensive plan provides comes from the fact that other benefits—such as income and estate tax savings—are garnered. The best way to protect yourself is to take advantage of tax and estate planning benefits available under law, which saves money and creates predictability and safety in your life. Thus, instead of being an expense, asset protection is actually a highly attractive endeavor that pays for itself.

One can only imagine how disappointing it must be for a doctor, who transfers the base of his wealth to his wife and children in fear of a lawsuit suing for his entire asset base, to ultimately have this transaction unwound because the court, rightly so, examines this transfer and detects badges of fraud.

This sort of plan has been used for years by physicians of all sorts. Unfortunately, it has been used in a vacuum of knowledge, which highlights the badges of fraud, and without the kind of planning that we find ourselves privy to today. One of the most important elements that this plan lacks is comprehensiveness. It does not show other benefits of the transfer or the kind of reasoning that the court wants to see in order to judge this action as nonfraudulent. It is clear to most practitioners that this problem is not limited to the medical community.

In many cases, persons who have fraudulently transferred are normal everyday businesspeople, lawyers, accountants—those people who you think would be aware of this problem. However, herein lies the greatest fallacy of this sort of work. The biggest problem in the field of asset protection is lack of knowledge. Most lawyers are painfully unaware of how this deal works, as are almost all accountants, financial planners, and other trained financial practitioners.

The lesson we learn from the trials and tribulations of the medical practitioner, the practicing lawyer, and the successful businessperson is that as they attempt to craft plans that will protect them from lawsuits and taxes, two critical errors are often made.

First, they try to craft the plan themselves with a very limited experiential base and little knowledge of the field. This approach virtually guarantees failure.

Second, when the vastly successful neurosurgeon

asks his trusted family attorney if such a plan can be done, strangely enough the answer is usually "no." One rather interesting course offered in law school is entitled "Fraudulent Conveyances" or "Fraudulent Transfers." What this course centers on are the methods by which one *may not* transfer property, not the methods by which one *can* transfer property in an effective manner. So unfortunately, the stock answer from most practitioners is that nothing can be done, which is wholly insufficient and many times is given by an advisor who is not really sure how it is done.

Furthermore, one must understand that in most cases, lawyers, like accountants and financial planners, may be somewhat familiar with a plan, but since they have no economic stake in the outcome of the exercise, they choose not to give advice, because should the plan in fact go bad, they would be held partially accountable.

Unfortunately, this leads us to the same problem that we examined before with the doctor transferring wealth: a plan that appears to be sufficient until it is tested.

So many times the answers to the question "Is your asset protection plan adequate and comprehensive?" are misleading. One answer is, "Well, yes, nothing has happened to it so far." Many times this answer is based on the simple fact that nothing has happened; the plan hasn't been tested yet and there has been no downside.

The solution to this problem is relatively simple. If one were to have an appendectomy, one would desire a trained professional. When something as simple as a tune-up on a car is done, most people turn to a professional. When tax forms are filed, the average citizen retains the services of a trained professional. There is no difference, philosophically speaking, between these endeavors and the formation of an asset protection plan. Now, the problem with this equation is that one immediately assumes that the place to go to find professional help is an attorney's office, and in many cases this is absolutely not true.

The person looking for a comprehensive plan should seek professional help to make sure that their asset protection plan is complete. This requires input from the areas of legal practitioners, accountants, registered investment advisors, and international tax experts, who can assist in the proper integration of domestic business activites with nondomestic business activities. If a planned bankruptcy is necessary, then a bankruptcy expert must be added to the list of professional helpers. It is the need for this combination of skills that makes it necessary to seek experts in asset protection, not just the services of an ordinary lawyer who may not be familiar with the field.

It is too often the case today that the issue of taxation is strictly a domestic one. Many American businesses are involved in international business affairs, which if properly structured could dramatically alter the taxation and income streams available from such activities. It is imperative that the international tax community be utilized to its fullest extent to effectuate the greatest savings and the greatest ability to control the timing of taxation for the taxpayer.

Many people today promote themselves as asset protection experts, yet what they do is provide a simple and insufficient solution to a very complex problem. For example, there are numerous seminars offered around the country promoting the use of family limited partnerships. Family limited partnerships are an excellent tool for asset protection. However, if used by itself and not as part of a comprehensive plan, the family limited partnership can fail to protect, and does in many cases due to the inability of a court to look at such a transaction without labeling it a sham.

It is imperative that the user understand the vacuum concept. In the vacuum, badges of fraud will be sought out and labeled as such, thereby enabling a court to either unravel the transaction or to create a heretofore unknown access to the corpus of the trust or partnership, which will avail the lien creditor of entry. Unfortunately, this comes at the worst possible time for the person attempting to protect their assets and results in forfeiture or confiscation. Attorneys are certainly adept at the drafting of these plans, but a more well-rounded organization is necessary for the proper implementation of such plans.

Comprehensive asset protection plans often involve the use of tax haven countries as places to establish offshore trusts, keep bank or securities accounts, and have investments managed.

One of the oft-neglected areas in the investment of an American's money in an "offshore" environment is what the actual investment scenario will be. Many times Americans enter a world with which they are unfamiliar and they do not recognize the significant risks that can be taken by investing in bonds, stocks, annuities, CDs, and so forth, in an unpredictable and unknown environment.

The domestic investor must be aware of the risks he is taking and the market conditions he is entering. More times than not, the less-than-professional investor should seek professional and accredited money management. If one were to turn to organizations like Jardine-Fleming in Hong Kong, Asset Protection Corporation in the United States, JML Swiss Investment Counsellors in Switzerland, or The Harris Organization in Panama, many times the unwieldy and unknown aspects of international investment would become easy and routine to deal with.

A decade or two ago, tax haven countries were used primarily by wealthy families to set up trusts for the grandchildren. As tax laws have changed, such simple solutions are generally no longer possible.

But today, the same countries and the same trust and corporate forms are being used to provide asset protection. The tax neutrality of the tax haven countries is ideal for this purpose, since there is no additional tax complication for the person seeking asset protection. Thus the tax haven business has slowly evolved into the asset protection business.

13

The truth is that wealthy families have had asset protection for decades using tested and perfected structures in stable jurisdictions such as Delaware and Switzerland. As asset protection has become something of a fad (it wasn't called asset protection back then), a lot of people are jumping on the latest gimmick promotion to come out—a distant sandbar with two palm trees, a law promising secrecy of bank accounts, and an American lawyer to hype it as the latest thing in asset protection.

It might work—but then again it might not. Since the asset protection business hasn't developed as part of the social fabric of the particular sandbar, the population and the local government really don't care if it works or not. Meanwhile, the registration fees for trusts and corporations enrich the country's treasury, and schemes that fail tend to get little publicity.

It is far preferable to stay with jurisdictions where the asset protection features have evolved as a fundamental part of the law and the local social and political structure. The Swiss law protecting insurance policies from seizure has been in effect since 1908—not to attract foreign business but because the Swiss wanted it to protect themselves. A Swiss court isn't going to look for excuses to carve exceptions out of the law.

Delaware has been protecting America's largest corporations and wealthiest families for decades. Panama has been a corporate management center since it became a country, because that business was an integral part of the commercial center that developed around the Panama Canal.

Asset protection is an art, not a science that can be replicated through experiments and demonstrations. This means that you will find contradictions in this book. One of the things to bear in mind when studying an art is that taste plays a role. The asset protection plan that suits the needs and prejudices of one person may not suit those of another. One investor may prefer to stay entirely domestic

14

using family limited partnerships in Delaware. Another may decide to add a Swiss annuity to that picture. Yet another may want to live in a rented apartment and have everything offshore in case the IRS comes to call.

Some may want to use a United States asset protection firm to implement a carefully structured plan combining tax, investment, and estate planning, while gaining asset protection as part of the package. This gives them the comfort of a fully defensible program based on United States legal and accounting advice. Others may decide to go directly offshore, purchasing a Swiss annuity and forming a British Virgin Islands corporation managed from Panama, without seeking United States planning and legal advice.

Most of these decisions are somewhat subjective and depend upon your personality and your personal experience as much as they do on the law. You have to go with the people, countries, and cultures that you feel comfortable with.

People frequently ask, "What is the best tax haven?" or "What is the best country in which to open a bank account?" There is no "best" answer—these things are very subjective and depend upon what you want to do.

2 Avoiding the Fraudulent Conveyance Trap

Integral parts of your financial planning are the ways and means legally available to protect your assets from potential judgment creditors, claims, liens, and attachments. Regardless of the operative specifics of the legal devices described, they all share a common objective: placing your property beyond the reach of others as securely as the law allows, while permitting you to retain if not the title at least some of the control and influence over that property and its income.

It is assumed that when you adopt any of these legal means of asset protection, your intention is just that—to protect your property from unforeseen depredations and to ensure a secure economic future for you and your family.

But consider the view from the other side of the table where your judgment creditor sits. What he or she sees is a person claiming to be "judgment proof" who holds no personal title to property that can satisfy a just debt or judgment, yet appears to live a comfortable life of wealth and ease. Understandably, your creditor and ultimately the court he invokes in aid of his appeal will want to know, "Where are the assets?"

The clear implication of that question is that you may have intentionally placed your assets in a sheltered

17

position where they continue to benefit you, but where creditors cannot get to them—in other words, that you have defrauded your creditors by concealing or transferring away your assets. An act, which to you was simply good business judgment, blossoms into allegations of fraud with potential civil and criminal significance. It is within this framework that I turn to a discussion of the law of fraudulent conveyances.

THE LAW OF FRAUDULENT CONVEYANCES

The word "conveyance" is nothing more than a legal term used to describe the act of transferring legal title to property from one person to another. We all understand the meaning of fraud. Put them together and you have the act of transferring title to property in order to deceive, cheat, or deprive someone of their legal right to that property.

Human nature being what it is, the problem of fraudulent conveyances is hardly something new. It was first dealt with in statutory form by the English with the "Statute of Elizabeth" in 1570. The basic elements of the law have changed little since.

In the United States, the law of fraudulent conveyances has been formalized in the Uniform Fraudulent Conveyances Act (UFCA) and the Uniform Fraudulent Transfers Act (UFTA), each of which has been adopted as law by about half of the states. Essentially, the law states that any transfer of property made with the intent to hinder, delay, or defraud creditors is voidable by those creditors at their option, even though the transfer may remain valid between the transferor and a "good faith" transferee.

A classic example of such chicanery is a debtor who deliberately sells property, then hides the proceeds of the sale in a Swiss bank account, hoping to enjoy the money at some future time. Meanwhile, his just debts go unpaid.

As you might imagine, in real life fraudulent conveyances are far more subtle and sophisticated—like transferring property and assets to a foreign asset protection trust, offshore corporation, limited partnership, or a spouse's living trust. This litany of asset protection devices should give you more than a hint—you too could face creditor charges of fraud, regardless of what your actual intent may have been at the time you transferred title to your assets to a seemingly impregnable asset protection device.

Any of these seemingly innocent actions can be alleged to fall within the definition of a "phony transfer," defined by Justice Brandeis of the U.S. Supreme Court in 1925 as a "transfer in trust," which in effect is "a transfer with absolute dominion reserved" by the transferor. In such a transfer, nothing changes realistically—the debtor signs over the title to some other entity but continues to use and enjoy the property, be it his business, mansion, or luxury yacht.

The late and notorious New York lawyer and social lion Roy Cohn, for example, conducted business from a well-appointed law office, lived in a luxurious West Side townhouse, had a yacht moored in the Hudson River, weekended at a country place in Greenwich, traveled elegantly in limousines and jetted around the world—yet he owed millions of dollars to creditors and the IRS and had absolutely no property titled in his name. His estate (what little there is of it) and his law firm (which the IRS has attached) are still embroiled in court battles—and will be for years to come.

INTENTIONAL FRAUD

The law of fraudulent conveyances requires as proof the showing of *subjective fraudulent intent* of the transferor—a very difficult burden for a creditor were it not for the development of a legal doctrine the courts have come to call "badges of fraud."

Obviously, no court has figured out a way to inspect

the contents of the mind of a person charged with fraud to ascertain without question what his or her intent may have been at the time of a transfer of assets. But since the time of Queen Elizabeth I and the original statute, courts have looked to certain evidences or marks of fraud and actions indicating true intention: so-called badges of fraud. These include conveyances made in secret, conveyances made while creditor litigation is pending, or conveyances made where the debtor retains possession and use of the property after it has been "transferred." Without regard to actual intent, a court may find *constructive fraud*, where a conveyance results in preventing the debtor from paying his debts, forcing him into insolvency, or removing sufficient capital to operate his business as debts come due.

There are other indicators of fraud, such as giving away property to a friend, spouse, or child at a time when the debtor is in a precarious financial condition; selling property for less than the true market value; or the debtor conveying away all of his assets at once, leaving him with little or nothing in his name.

The logical test in all these cases, as the law sees it, is to ask objectively whether or not the debtor's conduct is that of a person who is trying to cheat his creditors.

CREDITORS' REMEDIES

The importance of the answer to that question lies in the fact that a court can and will overturn a transfer of property if the answer is "yes." Depending upon the state's statute of limitations, the creditor has from two to six years to seek action, although under federal bankruptcy law it is one year.

When a creditor shows badges of fraud or evidence of constructive fraud, the burden of proof shifts to the debtor, who then must show he or she had no fraudulent intent.

Here is an important point to consider: the debt may

have been incurred prior to the transfer of assets, or it may have been incurred *after* the transfer of assets—a time sequence that is significant for those who thought their assets were secure because of their planning.

The creditor may be able to convince a court to issue a restraining order or an injunction against a pending transfer of assets, appoint a conservator who takes control of the debtor's property, or allow a judgment creditor to void the transfer and directly attach the property after it has been transferred, regardless of who or what holds title to it.

If the property subject to such an order is within the court's legal jurisdiction, any designs one may have had for asset protection disappear when the marshals arrive with the writs.

IN SUMMARY

Now that you understand the law of fraudulent conveyances, you can easily accept why its potential application to any of your proposed property transfers must be carefully considered. You can also appreciate why asset protection must be planned and executed well in advance of any possible financial trouble—not when the proverbial wolf is at the door.

3 False Asset Protection in Joint Ownerships

Joint ownership is probably the most prevalent form of family property ownership in the United States, with an estimated three-fourths of all real estate owned by married couples being held in some form of joint tenancy. Stocks, bonds, bank accounts, autos, boats, and numerous other items of personal property are also jointly owned, not just by husbands and wives but by virtually unlimited combinations of family and non-family multiparty ownerships—no doubt an accurate reflection of the enormous diversity of personal and business relationships existing in our modern society.

The question to consider is, "To what extent do the various forms of joint ownership provide the owners protection from creditors together and individually if, indeed, joint ownership affords any real creditor protection at all?"

JOINT TENANCY

A "joint tenancy" is when two or more people own property in equal and undivided shares, unless otherwise apportioned by agreement. The distinguishing feature is that upon the death of one joint tenant, the other joint tenant or tenants automatically receive ownership of the deceased joint tenant's share without having to go through probate. During life, a joint tenant can dispose of his or her joint interest without the consent of the other owner(s).

A joint tenancy is created when a property owner conveys to himself and another, or to two or more others, the property in described shares with an express declaration of joint tenancy. It offers no protection from creditors, and during a joint tenant's life, his or her interest is subject to attachment for debts. However, since joint tenancy includes the right of survivorship, the creditors of a deceased joint owner cannot reach the property as the title passes to the other joint tenant(s). Two exceptions are if the joint ownership was expressly created to defraud creditors of the deceased and for payment of federal or state taxes owed by the deceased.

In the case of joint bank accounts, joint ownership may or may not protect a joint tenant from attachment of the account for debts of the other joint owner, depending on the state and its case holdings. In many states, attachment of the account for debt is allowed, giving the creditor rights to the debtor's half of the account or, if the debtor contributed all or most of the money in the account, the creditor can obtain all of the funds.

Under federal bankruptcy law, the interest of a joint tenant is highly vulnerable when he or she files for bankruptcy, and creditors obtain increased collection rights against such property once bankruptcy is filed.

The bottom line is, as a possible asset protection device, holding title to property in joint tenancy does not offer much protection against creditors.

COMMUNITY PROPERTY STATES

In nine states—Arizona, California, Idaho, Louisiana, New Mexico, Nevada, Texas, Washington, and Wisconsin—a form of joint ownership by husband and wife known as "community property" is recognized by the law. This concept, which has origins in Spanish civil law, states that each spouse owns one-half of all jointly owned property and that their rights are approximately the same as the rights of joint tenants in giving them the ability to sell or encumber their interest during life. However, there is no survivorship at death, and the spouse's community property interest is passed to heirs through the courts or by will.

The laws of community property states vary greatly as to creditors' rights. Depending upon the state, creditors may be able to act against the spouses individually or jointly, or against the community property itself, depending on how community property is defined in that particular state. Creditors' rights depend on many factors, including which spouse obtained the credit, when it was obtained, whether it was obtained as an agent for the other spouse, whether it was to be an obligation against the community property itself, or whether it was to be a joint obligation.

It is enough to say that as a general rule, planned asset protection must be dealt with separately from marriage in such states.

TENANCY BY THE ENTIRETIES

Twenty-four states legally recognize "tenancy by the entireties," which is essentially a form of joint tenancy ownership of property available only to a husband and wife. As in the case of a joint tenancy, the right of survivorship goes to the remaining spouse automatically and without the need for probate, although estate taxes may be owed.

This form of joint ownership owes its existence to the common law theory that a man and woman united in matrimony became, in the eyes of the law, one person, that is, a "unity." According to this view, two people do not own the property, the single legal "person" created by the unity of marriage owns it. Because of this unity, neither party can convey away the property without the consent of the other or until one party dies or the marriage is dissolved.

Unless the property was jointly pledged by both parties to obtain a loan or other credit, as in a purchase money mortgage (used to finance the purchase of a property) or other mortgage, or unless some other debt was jointly incurred by both parties, upon the death of one party, the deceased individual's creditors have no rights to attach the property.

In some states like Massachusetts, a husband's creditors cannot force the sale of the property if it is a homestead as long as his wife is alive, but a lien can be placed against it, which may be satisfied eventually when she dies or sells the property after his death.

As far as asset protection is concerned, tenancy by the entireties will only protect the property to the extent that the debt sought to be enforced is incurred by only one spouse. If any debt is a joint debt of both husband and wife, the property is open to creditor attachment.

TENANCY IN COMMON

This is another form of joint ownership in which each joint tenant owns an equal or agreed upon share and has the right to sell or encumber that share without permission from the other tenants in common. There is no right of survivorship, and a deceased tenant's share goes to his heirs through the courts or can be disposed of by will.

This form of joint ownership offers no protection from creditors, who have the power to proceed against the interest of the tenant in common for the collection of debts. Creditors of one co-owner can either take title to the debtor's interest or force a partition and/or sale of the property.

4 Traditional Judgment-Proofing Techniques

Both federal and state governments, by constitutional or statutory provisions, have adopted certain defined exemptions that protect the property of a debtor from a judgment creditor. These exemptions are rooted in public policy considerations seeking to protect the debtor as the head of a household, his family, or his attainment of other social and political goals judged by policy makers to outweigh a creditor's right to collect a debt.

THE HOMESTEAD EXEMPTION

One of the most significant safeguards a debtor has is the *homestead exemption*, which is allowed under the laws of all but a few states. The first of these laws was enacted in Texas in 1839, and although they vary greatly in their liberality and application, all have the objective of preserving a place in which a debtor and his or her family can continue to live, regardless of their economic difficulties. Under federal bankruptcy law, the state homestead exemption law applicable to the person filing bankruptcy in that state must be honored.

The exemption applies only to real estate owned and occupied as a primary residence by a debtor, who is the head of a household, and his family—usually a single-family home, but in many states extending to condominiums, co-op apartments, and even mobile homes. Some states now make the exemption available to single unmarried persons as well.

In order to be protected by this exemption, it is necessary to claim it under state law usually by executing some form of written declaration, which in some states must be recorded in the official land records. In most states, the exemption can be claimed even after a judgment creditor has had an execution levied against the property. Several states do not exempt the home property from debts acquired before the homestead was purchased.

The value of the exemption varies according to state law, which sets a stated maximum figure, usually in the range of $1,000 to $20,000, or expresses the exemption in land area terms. New Jersey allows none, Utah very little, but states such as Texas and Florida are well known for their liberality on this point.

Texas allows an exemption of 200 rural acres and a home without regard to value. In cities it allows land and improvements acquired for $10,000 or less without regard to appreciated value. When the late John Connolly, former Texas governor and U.S. Secretary of the Treasury, was forced to file for personal bankruptcy, he auctioned off all sorts of personal property, but continued to live on his ranch, which was worth many millions of dollars.

Written into the Florida constitution is a similar exemption, which protects 160 acres in rural areas or one-half acre in urban areas, plus the residence located thereon, regardless of actual worth. Because of the value of Florida real estate, the state has become a mecca for wealthy persons facing financial problems who move there, purchase multimillion-dollar horse farms or waterfront residences, then file personal bankruptcy, secure in the protection of their new "homestead," however luxurious it may be. Repeated attempts to tighten the law have met a dead end in the state legislature.

In states where the homestead exemption is less generous, nothing prevents the forced sale of a home to pay a judgment creditor, although the homeowner is allowed to retain the dollar amount of the exemption before the balance goes toward satisfaction of the debt owed to the creditor.

The moral of this interesting story: check out Florida or Texas if you are in personal financial trouble and can afford to sink a large chunk of your remaining capital into a very nice home. Don't forget to have a spouse who can afford the utilities and upkeep.

LIFE INSURANCE

Life insurance should be an essential part of estate and asset protection planning. In many instances, the proceeds from a life insurance policy constitute the largest or second largest (after the value of a person's home) asset in an estate.

Since 1840, when the first such law was adopted, every state has approved statutory exemptions for life insurance policies from the collection of debts owed by the policy owner, and most states extend that exemption to the proceeds due to a qualified beneficiary of such a policy. In states that do not grant exemptions to the policy beneficiary, the creation of a life insurance trust with the same beneficiary will solve this problem and may also provide some tax advantages.

The life insurance exemption usually covers the cash surrender value of the policy as well. Although the justification for the exemption is said to be protection for the dependents of the insured debtor, most laws allow nondependent beneficiaries to have the exemption.

If you are in a financial position to do so comfortably, paying in full the premium on your life insurance policy in an appropriate amount, which is payable to your spouse and/or children as alternate beneficiaries, is one way to protect them and park some of your capital where it can't be reached by creditors.

RETIREMENT INCOME

Federal and state statutes also exempt certain types of retirement income paid to a judgment debtor from garnishment or other judicial processes ordinarily available to creditors. These exemptions include Social Security retirement and disability payments, welfare aid to families with dependent children (AFDC), and many states also include government payments due to blindness, disability, or benefits for the elderly.

Federal law also exempts certain specified amounts of basic income and other federal payments under the Consumer Credit Protection Act, and under both federal bankruptcy laws and the Employee Retirement Income Security Act of 1974 (ERISA) qualified private pensions generally cannot be garnished for debt. "Qualified" refers to any private plan in which the pension beneficiary is unable to pledge or otherwise alienate his or her interest in the plan—a plan that is, in effect, a "spendthrift trust."

The ERISA exemptions also extend to so-called Keogh plans if they are organized with an independent trustee as opposed to the beneficiary acting as his or her own trustee. While there is no federal protection for independent retirement accounts or annuities (IRAs), many state laws include them in the exemption granted to all other pension plans.

One problem in using a pension plan as an asset protection device occurs if the pension beneficiary files for bankruptcy. This exposes the value of the pension to creditors' claims and possible attachment. There has also been a recent trend in state court decisions allowing attachment of pension plans for limited claims such as

30

alimony and child support, and when legal conflicts arise between the employee entitled to the pension and the employer paying the pension.

GIFTS

Giving gifts of money or property during your lifetime is one way to protect those assets from probate and estate taxes. However, gifts in excess value of $10,000 in one year may subject you to federal and state gift taxes, so a tax advisor should be consulted as to the consequences.

Remember that under the law of fraudulent conveyances, a person may not simply give away his or her assets to avoid creditors who may be seeking payment of debts. Nor can one make gifts that cause him or her to fall into a precarious financial condition, thus jeopardizing creditors' rights, even though there may be paper assets left that create the appearance of solvency, such as shares in a business that is actually worthless.

5 Using Corporations to Limit Liability

The first thought that comes to mind when the word "incorporating" is mentioned is the legal principle known as "limited liability."

Individuals who form a corporation to conduct business legally insulate themselves and their real and personal property from any debts, lawsuits, and other claims that arise against the business. Instead of being personally liable, except in rare instances, the law holds the entity known as the "corporation" and its assets responsible for such claims—not the people who manage and own that corporation, or officers, directors, and shareholders.

It is this central feature of the corporate form of doing business—protection against personal liability—that makes it so attractive for persons wishing to shield their assets from possible lawsuits, debts, or other potential demands.

What kind of business or other activity especially needs the protection of a corporation? The short answer is, any activity where there is a potential for liability. This is true if you have one or more employees; if you frequently interact with the public, clients, patients, and other businesses; if you are involved in joint ventures; if you engage in any hazardous activity; or if you share

33

space or facilities with other professionals with whom you are otherwise not associated. If you are currently acting on your own in any of these business situations and are unprotected as the sole proprietor, you could be one lawsuit away from financial ruin.

TAX REASONS FOR INCORPORATING

Asset protection is not the only good reason for forming a business corporation. You can also use a corporation to increase your available cash by paying minimal taxes and provide you with personal benefits.

Establishing a corporation allows officers and directors to finance many expenses through the company. For example, you can create a corporate health and medical expense reimbursement plan entirely paid for by the company, tax deductible as a business expense, and with tax-free benefits to those included in the plan. The corporation can also establish and pay for pension and other benefits for its officers. Other necessary expenditures that may be treated as legitimate business expenses include the purchase of automobiles, equipment, and travel.

Although the value of these goods and services has to be included in the recipient's gross income, they are tax deductible business expenses for the corporation, and as such reduce net income and, therefore, company taxes. It is also less costly to include the value received in gross income rather than to purchase the same things with your after-tax income. Officers can also obtain more personal tax-advantaged cash from the business by buying business assets themselves and then leasing them to the corporation.

A shrewd investor will also consider shifting at least part of his or her stock portfolio to his or her corporation for management and investment purposes. Corporations are allowed to deduct from gross income 70 percent of the dividends received from other United States corporations that are subject to U.S. income taxes.

That deduction rises to 80 percent of dividends received if your corporation owns 20 percent of the stock of the payor corporation and more if the corporation is considered to be "affiliated" as defined by the IRS Tax Code. (However, that would rule out a Subchapter "S" status, as discussed below.)

With the top personal individual income tax rate now substantially above the top corporate income tax rate, there is an incentive for owners of regular (non-S) corporations to take less money in salary and retain more for the corporation to invest. The company can accumulate up to $250,000 in corporate earnings without incurring a tax penalty and more if it can be justified for anticipated needs. Otherwise, the corporation is hit with a 39.6 percent tax on the excess accumulation.

In addition to health and pension benefits, tax breaks, and limited liability, there are other solid reasons for incorporation:

- Ownership of shares is more easily transferred to family members as gifts or by sale to others than by bequests at death, and transfers can be restricted in a closed corporation to a limited group when working together is the objective.
- Since the corporation has a life of its own ("in perpetuity"), the death of officers or directors does not interrupt the business.
- Many businesses give corporate discounts for goods and services, such as airfare and other forms of travel, and this can add up to significant savings.

SUBCHAPTER S CORPORATIONS

The one tax problem presented by the corporate form is double taxation, first by imposition of the tax on corporate income, then by the personal income tax levied on

35

dividends paid to shareholders, salaries, and other payments made to officers and directors of the company. Although it is unusual, the federal government has in this instance provided relief for this double taxation problem in an effort to promote small businesses.

Subchapter S of the IRS Tax Code allows a small business corporation to elect to have the undistributed taxable income of the corporation taxed as personal income for the shareholders, thus avoiding any corporate income tax. If the shareholders are your children, their reduced income status will mean still lower income taxes. Corporate losses can also be claimed directly by the shareholders. In this sense, the Subchapter S tax status is like that of a general partnership, but it retains the corporate liability protection that such a partnership does not enjoy.

A small business corporation can qualify for Subchapter S treatment if:

- it is properly incorporated under state law;
- it has 35 or fewer shareholders;
- it has only one class of stock;
- it has shareholders who qualify as IRS-recognized individuals, estates, or trusts (other shareholding corporations or partnerships do not qualify);
- it is not affiliated with another corporation, meaning it does not hold 80 percent or more ownership of another corporation.

THE CORPORATE SOLUTION

There are at least five good reasons to incorporate your business or profession:

1) to limit your personal liability;
2) to cut your tax bill;

3) to centralize management;
4) to permit the easy transfer of interests and ownership;
5) for the ease of doing business.

The magic legal solution that provides all of these benefits is a "corporation"—an entity that the U.S. Supreme Court has defined as "an artificial being, invisible, intangible, and existing only in contemplation of law."

A more explicit definition of a corporation is a legal "person" composed of one or more natural persons, which is entirely separate and distinct from the individual or individuals who compose it.

However abstract the corporation may be in theory, in fact, its recognition in law gives it great power. Much of the business and trade in the United States is conducted in the corporate form, ranging in size from giants like General Motors and AT&T to your local "mom and pop" gas station/convenience store.

Since corporations are entities "in contemplation of law," their formation, structure, and powers are governed by the laws of the 50 states and the District of Columbia, in any one of which you can start a company.

Even though the corporate business form has been in use for centuries and the American Bar Association has adopted a Model Business Corporation Act, the individual corporation laws of each state still vary greatly. For example, in one state the law says the duration of a corporation's legal existence is 25 years, in another it is 99 years, in many others it is perpetual. The law of the state in which you choose to incorporate will govern what you can and cannot do as a corporation.

There is no federal law allowing the creation of private national corporations as such, but there are federal corporations created by act of Congress, which are usually quasi-public companies with government involvement such as the U.S. Postal Service,

Amtrak, or the well-known FDIC (Federal Deposit Insurance Corporation).

State laws also allow the creation of special government corporations, usually by act of the legislature, such as municipal corporations or quasi-governmental bodies for designated purposes such as constructing and managing public works like school districts, harbor and port facilities, or water conservation districts. These government corporations are totally distinct from private corporations, which we are discussing here.

CORPORATE STRUCTURE

Corporations have the advantage of a defined centralized management structure with consolidated control, flexibility, permanency, and limited liability for shareholders. Corporate powers are so all-inclusive that they are almost coextensive with the powers a human individual can exercise in business.

The owners of a corporation are the shareholders who own stock in the company. The board of directors manage the business, and the officers—president, vice president, secretary, and treasurer—are responsible for day-to-day operation. Most state laws minimally require this basic corporate structure.

Be aware that if state law allows, small corporations, often called "close" or "closely held" corporations, can operate with only one or two stockholders, directors, and officers, several or all of whom may be the same person. Many states like Delaware, New York, and Nevada allow one-person corporations. This minimum requirement satisfies what sounds like complicated requirements of state law—mostly paperwork—and makes a company relatively easy to run.

A stock corporation is one that issues capital stock divided into shares held by the owners of the corporation, known as shareholders, and is authorized by law to pay its profits to the shareholders in the form of dividends. Generally, stock corporations, also called "close" or "privately owned" companies whose shares are not listed or traded on a stock exchange, are usually exempt from federal laws controlling the issuance and registration of securities.

THE INCORPORATION PROCESS

The term "incorporation" describes the process by which a corporation is formed under state law.

Assuming the purpose of your business is known, including of course asset protection, the choice of a name is in order. Both the purpose and name of the business must be included in the "articles of incorporation," a basic document required for filing with the appropriate state agency—the agency name varies from state to state. Usually, registration is with the office of the secretary of state, the corporation counsel, the department of revenue, the commerce department, or a state agency with a similar title.

When you choose a corporate name, you may discover that certain words are not available for general use in corporate names since they denote specially licensed occupations or activities. These include titles such as attorney, bank, trust, cooperative, doctor, police. Each of these special businesses has its own incorporation methods described in the state laws governing that field of activity. Often, such groups qualify for incorporation as "professional corporations" or "professional associations," which gives them limited liability but also means they must have special qualifications to obtain a license.

Most state laws require that your company name include words that notify the public of your corporate form, such as incorporated, corporation, limited, company, or variations of these words.

Once it is certain your corporate name is available for

use—that it is not the same as or similar to another name—the articles of incorporation can be written and filed with the state.

The articles should set out the names of the original incorporators (usually three are required), purpose of the corporation, directors' meeting requirements, number and classes of shares to be issued, location of the office, name of the registered agent, and other major details.

After the articles are filed and any corporate occupation taxes are paid, the corporate existence is a matter of public record, and you are ready to do business.

MULTIPLE CORPORATIONS

It is not unusual in some situations for a person to create two or more corporations designed to handle different aspects of his or her business or professional activities. This might be done for partial claims protection, especially if some part of the overall business operation involves a particularly hazardous or liability-prone activity. Or a business with interstate activity might be incorporated separately in two different states to guard against the possibility of some future problem in one of the states, which would not impair operations in both. In some cases, one company might be used for business operations, while the other holds title to the plant and equipment. There are many possibilities all looking toward maximum asset protection.

You may even decide that creating a "holding company" is in order—a corporation formed expressly to own and manage other corporations ("subsidiaries") which are part of your business operations. In such situations, the holding company usually owns at least 80 percent of the subsidiary companies' stock.

ORGANIZATION AND OPERATION

Once the state has officially recognized your corporation, the first step is to hold an organizational meeting to elect the board of directors and officers, adopt bylaws, price initial stock values, and approve contracts of employment and other initial start-up authorizations, such as opening a company bank account. The board is required to meet at least once a year for the election of officers and directors and other business. Full and accurate minutes of all meetings must be kept, both to satisfy the law and protect the corporate status.

Like other legal entities, corporations have the power to hold title to property, enter into contracts, sue and be sued, and do all things necessary for its business. Corporations exist in perpetuity or until they are dissolved by either the act of the directors or by the state— the latter usually occurs after failure to pay annual operating fees or taxes or file required reports.

Since your company is likely to be a closely held corporation, it is important to make it clear to the general public and creditors that they are dealing with a corporation, not you personally. Failure to make known the use of the corporate business form can result in the loss of limited liability protection for individual officers and directors, thus negating the whole purpose of the incorporation. This publicity rule also applies to any agents or employees of the corporation and should always govern their conduct.

Using corporate checking accounts, stationary, business cards, and documents, which are always signed in a corporate capacity, will protect you and the company and allow people to understand they are doing business with a corporation, not an individual acting under a trade or company name.

Maintaining the corporate identity is especially important when obtaining financing for a new business, which often requires personal guarantees for loans unless the corporation is well capitalized. All loan documents should clearly reflect whether it is the corporation or the individual who is primarily responsible for repayment. Officers should always indicate their official company position when signing on its behalf by following their name with their corporate title or adding a phrase such as "For the XYZ Co., Inc."

PIERCING THE CORPORATE VEIL

Officers, directors, and controlling shareholders have a general fiduciary duty of loyalty and care, which should govern all their corporate conduct. Unless they breach that duty by gross negligence or acting in bad faith, they usually will have no liability to third parties. Third parties have to show personal wrongful conduct on the part of a company official or director to hold them responsible—actions that support application of the legal doctrine known as "piercing the corporate veil."

There are possible breaches in the wall of personal liability provided by incorporation, and for your asset safety you should know how these exceptions come about.

Certain acts of directors and officers may be grounds for a company creditor to ask a court to pierce the corporate veil—which means just what it says. For example, if the corporation cannot pay a creditor's proven debt or a litigant's claim, the individuals behind the corporation can be held personally responsible for its obligations, even though they have given no personal guarantees. This can happen when:

- corporate debt is knowingly incurred when the company is already insolvent;
- required annual shareholders or board of directors meetings are not held, or other corporate formalities are not observed;
- corporate records, especially minutes of direc-

tors meetings, are not properly or adequately maintained;

- shareholders remove unreasonable amounts of funds from the corporation, endangering its financial stability;
- there is a pattern of consistent nonpayment of dividends or payment of excessive dividends;
- there is a general commingling of actions or funds of the corporation and those belonging to the person or persons who control the corporation;
- there is a failure to maintain separate offices, or the company has little other business and is used only as a facade for the activities of the dominant shareholder.

In order to maintain personal limited liability, it is essential these described actions be avoided. Courts in recent years have delighted in finding new excuses for holding directors, officials, and shareholders liable for corporate liabilities. Other activities that courts have found to be the basis for personal liability have included improper corporate guarantees of loans or contracts benefiting an officer, timing of the sale of a controlling interest for self benefit, profiting from inside information, transactions with other businesses that can be held to be conflicts of interest, unreasonable loans to company officials, and extension of unwarranted credit.

Directors are generally held to a higher standard of duty than officers because they hold the ultimate controlling power, including the election or removal of officers.

Without any need for the IRS to rend the corporate veil, directors and officers can also be held liable for federal taxes owed by the corporation—both corporate income tax on the annual business net profit and unpaid payroll taxes for employees.

As an extra asset protection arrangement, experts recommend that in a closely held family corporation, only one spouse, husband or wife, serves as a director, thus limiting potential family liability in the event the corporate veil is pierced by adverse legal action. One-spouse operations are possible in states where one-person corporations are permitted, such as Delaware.

WHICH STATE FOR INCORPORATION?

If your corporation is intended as an operating business in a specific state, usually the one in which you live or intend to do business, that usually is the best state in which to incorporate.

Any business that incorporates in one state and does business in another is required to "qualify to do business" in the other state. This means formally registering, paying a franchise or other initial tax, filing annual reports, and paying annual taxes in the second state—all because yours is a "foreign corporation" chartered in another state. In other words, the red tape is doubled by incorporating in one state and doing business in another. If you have a multistate business operation, this is an acceptable burden, but if not, this places a premium on incorporating in the state in which you are located and doing business.

Delaware: The Company State

Why have so many people heard that no matter where you live, Delaware is the state in which to incorporate your business?

Why is it that a large percentage of the publicly held corporations in America—and more than half of the Fortune 500 companies—are incorporated in the state of Delaware, the 49th smallest state in geographic area (2,045 square miles) and only 47th in population (less than 700,000 in the 1990 census) but the biggest in the incorporation business?

44

The answer is simple. Smart businesspeople go where they get the best deal, and Delaware is the one state that has long formulated its tax, commercial, and banking laws with the specific objective of attracting business from all over the nation. Unlike some other states—New York, for example—which have driven business away by imposing onerous tax and regulatory burdens, Delaware official policy has always been "corporation-friendly."

What Delaware incorporation means for some types of small businesses, regardless of the state in which their officers or activities may be located, is an optimal ease and ability to conduct corporate affairs with minimal government interference and taxation. The Delaware laws may be far more favorable than those in your own state, and it is worth checking to be sure.

The state of Delaware's Division of Incorporations officially suggests these advantages of incorporating in their state:

- The franchise tax compares favorably with that of any other state, and there is no corporate income tax for companies conducting their business outside the state.
- Shares of stock owned by persons outside the state are not subject to taxation.
- There is no sales, personal property, or intangible property tax for Delaware corporations not doing business in the state.
- Shares of stock that are part of the estate of a deceased nonresident are exempt from the state inheritance tax law.
- The state's courts have an established record of liberally construing the corporation law, which gives investors confidence in the security of their investment.
- Corporate directors have greater statutory legal protection from personal liability than in other states.

45

- There is no minimum capital requirement necessary to form a corporation.
- If you wish, your identity as the owner of a corporation may remain anonymous, and a single individual may incorporate.
- A Delaware corporation may hold its annual meetings, keep its books and records, and have its principal office in another state.

If you are thinking of forming a Delaware corporation, you should check the method, costs, name availability, reporting requirements, franchise and annual taxes, and filing fees in your own state associated with qualifying to do business there as a foreign corporation, which you will have to do if you incorporate in Delaware. It may cost you less to incorporate in your own state, and your state's corporation laws might tend to be as liberal as those in Delaware, although few are.

If you want to form a one-person corporation, check to see what your state law says. Many states require a minimum of three incorporators and three directors, and some don't allow anonymity for the true owner as Delaware does.

For information on a highly recommended national service that can form a corporation for you in any state, write to Incorporation Information Package, 818 Washington Street, Wilmington, DE 19801.

Watch Out for the Nevada Promotions

Once you're operating your small business, you should seriously consider the advantages of incorporating in Nevada. Nevada is one of several states that has no corporate income tax. In addition, it has no state personal income tax and no franchise tax. Many large corporations use Nevada for warehousing because there is no inventory tax. This may seem beyond the reach of a small business, but if you organize your business as a

Nevada corporation, you may then contract with a local warehousing and fulfillment service to process and ship orders from Nevada.

Already such companies as Citibank and Porsche North America have moved their corporate headquarters to Nevada. For as little as $2,500 you can enjoy the same advantages as these corporate giants.

For many companies the most important reason to incorporate in Nevada is that there is no state income tax. If you live in a high-tax state, this can be crucial. In California, for example, corporations pay a minimum of $9,600 on every $100,000 of taxable income.

Tax Avoidance

If minimizing taxes is your concern, your strategy should be to form a Nevada corporation and arrange for the profits to accumulate there rather than in the high tax state in which you presently do business.

This is easier than you may think. Suppose you run a small company and have some major element of the business that can be handled from Nevada or a service that can be contracted for through the Nevada corporation. If you do this with a service, it is important that the entire service is not performed in the high-tax state, in which case the Nevada corporation is subject to the same taxes in that state as any local corporation. Your sales representative travels a 10-state area, so you make the Nevada corporation your distributor for those 10 states and pay his salary out of that corporation. His official base is now Nevada. You pay your Nevada corporation a sufficient commission to keep most of the profits in Nevada instead of the state where your business is physically headquartered.

Or you could contract for sales management services from the Nevada corporation, pay it a fixed fee, and it pays your salesman. You tell your salesman that he is being transferred to a new employer. He still gets the same

47

salary, and he still does the same job at the same pay. The only difference to him is that his paycheck comes from a different issuer. Your fee to the Nevada sales management company might be $75,000. Supposing that you pay the Nevada corporation an extra $47,000 in management fees over what your salesman was previously paid, your net profit is zero. Oddly enough, that's good news. Zero profit means zero corporate income tax in your high-tax jurisdiction. Now you have $47,000 of profit at zero taxes in your Nevada corporation. Best of all, it's perfectly legal. All you have to do is make certain that the accounting and management of the sales company are being done through the Nevada corporation and that all sales are booked and invoiced accordingly.

This general method of transferring income and profit from high-tax jurisdictions to low-tax jurisdictions is common. It will work for just about any goods or services your business requires, other than those of a purely local nature.

Note that a Nevada corporation will help reduce only your state taxes. Federal taxes apply in all states. However, you could create a third company in a tax-free jurisdiction outside the United States. Then you could potentially escape federal taxes as well. (But before doing that, it is important to get good accounting advice so that you don't have an argument with the IRS over "transfer pricing." Transfer pricing is a tax term referring to the price at which related corporations buy and sell goods to each other.)

Lawsuit Protection

Many promoters of Nevada corporations try to sell you on using a Nevada corporation for lawsuit protection. Unfortunately, most of the information being given out is not only inaccurate, it is positively dangerous. Generally, it is based on hiding your ownership of the Nevada corporation. Keeping your ownership private and confidential is fine and may reduce the risk of a lawsuit because you don't appear to be a financially attractive target, but actually hiding your assets in litigation is fraud, and lying about your assets in a court proceeding is perjury. A quiet public appearance is one thing, but don't let the people trying to sell you a Nevada corporate package lure you into inadvertently committing a crime. It is you, not the corporate agents, who will be facing a prison sentence, and saying you got your legal advice from a corporate promoter's brochure is not a good defense.

Financial Privacy

Nevada corporate promotion literature usually stresses the fact that Nevada does not require public disclosure of corporate shareholders. They conveniently forget to tell you that neither does any other state in the United States! In all states, the officers and directors are a matter of public record. Any corporation provides privacy to the extent that to determine who the shareholders are, a court action involving either the corporation or the individual is necessary. But if a court in your home state has jurisdiction over you because of a lawsuit, all of your holdings have to be disclosed. (There are ways to protect those assets with trusts, but thinking your concealed ownership of a corporation in Nevada or in any other state is asset protection is foolhardy and reckless.)

Another claim a few of the Nevada promoters make is that Nevada allows bearer shares. It doesn't, and federal tax law prohibits the issuance of bearer shares by corporations in the United States.

Nevada state law requires that all Nevada corporations retain the services of a resident agent in the state who must have on file the name and address of the person who holds the stock ledger. But the resident agent is not required to keep the ledger himself. Again, contrary to what the promoters tell you, this is identical to the corporation law of the other 49 states and the District of Columbia.

Corporation laws in all states are relatively uniform—it is the tax laws that create the interesting differences.

Nevada promoters will tell you that there are no minimum capital requirements, which is true of about 40 states, and the rest require a very nominal amount like $500 or $1,000. They'll also tell you that one person can hold all corporate offices and be the sole director, but almost every state now has this feature.

One Nevada promoter's brochure even claims that legally you can make up any name you wish as director of the corporation, citing the common law rule that "a person may use any name providing it is not for a fraudulent purpose." Fortunately, most of the corporate brochures don't go this far, for this is again very dangerous advice about an often quoted but completely misconstrued concept of common law. Using a different name in your role as director of a corporation—in any jurisdiction—will not only be construed as a fraudulent act but will convert your otherwise legitimate corporate business activities to fraud. Many states do have a common law principle that you may use any name—*if* you consistently and publicly adopt that name for all purposes. Most states require this public adoption by court order, and a few states make it a criminal offense to use a name not on your birth certificate unless it has been changed by court order. So don't fall for this one just because somebody told you that you could legally do it. The very fact that you are only using the name to hide your directorship in the Nevada corporation is overwhelming evidence of fraud in any state. You could jeopardize your entire business—and even if you are not prosecuted, the resulting stench, should it come out, could destroy the reputation of your business. Would you want to do business with somebody who ran their business under a false name? You'd certainly question his integrity and honest intentions.

The tax savings afforded by a Nevada corporation

make it a tool worth considering—even if you have never incorporated before. Needless to say, this attractive combination of benefits has spawned a whole new service industry to assist you. Many of the widely advertised corporate formation services are very good. But remember, they are only corporate formation agents, not lawyers or accountants.

One last word of advice. The most common pitfall in using a Nevada corporation the way I have described is the temptation to cut corners. It is not enough merely to pretend to do business in Nevada. You run the risk of losing all your benefits if the books aren't in order, or if the board doesn't meet regularly to approve whatever the company is doing, or if the minutes of those board meetings are not up-to-date, or any other legal technicality has not been properly attended to and officially documented. But as a carefully and prudently run business, you can be assured that all the advantages I have discussed are yours to keep.

A Nevada corporation can be formed by the incorporating service whose information package I mentioned earlier. But despite the heavy advertising for Nevada corporations in the last few years, Delaware offers the same advantages with a better image and decades more experience.

6 Using a Secret Foreign Corporation

As our world becomes smaller and few businesses are local or even strictly national, there is an increasing need for internationalization. We think, plan, and work with an eye toward expanding our horizons both at home and abroad. The use of a corporate vehicle as a means of this expansion is nothing new. What is new and what must become second nature to people of all types is the idea of foreign corporations.

A domestic corporation will no longer satisfy everyone's needs. The average businessperson today is far more sophisticated than the businessperson of 10 to 15 years ago. Corporate structuring and planning have achieved higher levels of complexity than ever before, while the need for anonymity remains strong.

Entrepreneurs must keep pace and be constantly on the lookout for new ways to profit. One way is to have a clear understanding of the characteristics of foreign corporations and how they may be put to use advantageously.

Foreign corporations are used outside of the place of incorporation for a seemingly endless variety of activities, including trading, trade financing, holding assets, manufacturing, and tax minimization. They are often used for trading with or within countries where satisfactory local, commercial, or corporate law is deficient or absent. Joint ventures often use foreign corporations when the participants are from different countries and prefer to incorporate in a jurisdiction neutral to all of the parties.

Foreign corporations can also serve to isolate or separate activities, assets, or profit centers for tax, accounting, or liability reasons. Where assets are cumbersome or expensive to transfer, like patents, copyrights, or trademarks, it is sometimes feasible to have separate corporations hold such assets, which allows the individual to transfer shares in the corporation rather than the asset itself.

In some cases, a foreign corporation, recognized as a citizen or national of the place of incorporation, may confer a trade advantage or help avoid a disadvantage. It may also be used as an integral part of a trust structure.

Certain countries seek to make it attractive to incorporate in their jurisdiction, even when activities are to be conducted elsewhere. In fact, there are so many "tax efficient" jurisdictions that an initial problem for most users is how to select from the available options.

When selecting a place to incorporate, most professionals consider the following criteria:

1) the legal and political attitude of the jurisdiction toward commercial activities;
2) features of the corporate law that facilitate incorporation and continuing management;
3) the level and speed of service obtainable in and from the jurisdiction; and
4) cost.

Generally, a desirable jurisdiction is politically neutral, follows a policy of free trade, does not interfere with the commercial activities of corporations established there, and is politically accepting of other countries and places with which the corporation may be trading.

Formal diplomatic recognition as well as commercial

recognition and acceptability are important. Commercial recognition is a feature of an offshore jurisdiction that is earned. Use of a jurisdiction in financial transactions allows banks to become familiar and more comfortable with its legal system and forms of corporate documentation. Most popular jurisdictions have a legal system derived from a major western country and greatly favor corporations that are nonresident in nature. Most professionals prefer their western style legislation since it provides a familiar basis for legal interpretation and facilitates understanding of their laws in international practice, particularly in developed countries. In addition, inherent in the western tradition is the protection of private property and the promotion of international trade.

In order to be successful, corporate law must give corporations the legal capacity to conduct all forms of commercial activity anywhere in the world, allow for a simple management structure and provide them with broad financial powers. In addition, corporations should be highly confidential and have minimal requirements for maintaining their legal existence in compliance with the laws of the place of incorporation. All jurisdictions have at least two maintenance requirements:

1) maintaining an agent for the service of process,
2) paying an annual franchise fee or tax.

In jurisdictions patterned on U.S. law, there are generally no further requirements. This should be considered when choosing between a United States or United Kingdom style jurisdiction.

United Kingdom style jurisdictions usually require annual filings listing directors and officers and at a minimum request that the annual accounts of the corporation be maintained in the jurisdiction. Such accounts may be subject to review by the registrar, but in some cases they need not be filed. This is one major advantage of United States style jurisdictions over those following the United Kingdom model.

Finally, formation services should be easy to obtain and should guarantee corporate existence in one or two working days. The level of service varies between jurisdictions. There can also be variation within the jurisdiction in a situation where there is competition between rival franchises engaging in the business of incorporating offshore companies. An organization that offers a wide range of services undoubtedly is best equipped with trained personnel to handle questions informally and has a larger base of experience upon which to draw when answering questions.

Incorporation fees may vary from $575 to $3,500. Minimum annual fees vary from $350 to over $1,000 depending on the jurisdiction and the local maintenance requirements. There should be no other mandatory fees or charges upon incorporation or for the maintenance of the corporation.

This summary is only a brief introduction to the use and features of foreign corporations and the characteristics of a typical offshore corporate statute. One of the best sources of help in setting up offshore trusts and corporations is Marc Harris, an American certified accountant who has a large practice in Panama. Harris completed the certified public accountancy examination at the age of 18. He is believed to be the youngest person in the United States to have passed the examination. He also holds a master's degree in business administration from Columbia University in New York.

He opened his Panamanian firm in 1985 after consulting for the accounting firm of Ernst & Whinney. His services are highly recommended because he can create and administer offshore corporations and trusts in complete compliance with U.S. laws. Often an American client uses a tax-haven-based advisor who knows the local laws but is not familiar with American tax law requirements and technicalities, and the client eventually gets into trouble. Marc Harris has a unique ability to bridge the two worlds for his clients. Although based in Panama, he can create and administer corporations and trusts that are registered in all of the popular tax havens.

For more information, please write to the firm of Marc M. Harris, Inc., Attn: Traditional Client Services, Estafeta El Dorado, Apartado Postal 6-1097, Panama 6, Panama.

For the most detailed information on tax havens and forming corporations in tax haven countries, order *The Tax Haven Report* from Scope International Ltd., Box AS125, Forestside House, Forestside, Rowlands Castle, Hants., PO9 6EE, Great Britain. The price is $125 (U.S.), which includes airmail postage worldwide, and they accept Visa or MasterCard. If you want it sent by surface mail, the price is $100. They will also send a free catalog of all of their special reports.

If you want to gain a good understanding of how the government views tax havens, University Microfilms International is now making available *Tax Havens and Their Uses by United States Taxpayers* by Richard Gordon through its Books On Demand program. Frequently referred to as "The Gordon Report," this is a 1981 U.S. Treasury Department study prepared at the request of Congress, which gives considerable detail and examples of the uses of tax havens. Although it has been out of print for over a decade, anyone interested in tax havens who has not studied the work will still find plenty of useful information in it. Copies can be ordered through booksellers or directly from University Microfilms International, 300 North Zeeb Road, Ann Arbor, MI 48106-1346. Prices are $67.30 softbound or $73.30 hardbound. The UMI catalog number of the book is AU00435, and UMI accepts Visa or MasterCard.

OPENING A FOREIGN
CORPORATE BANK ACCOUNT

The opening of a corporate bank account, seemingly a simple task, in fact requires considerable thought and preparation. When opening a foreign corporate bank account in particular, one should give attention to a number of factors.

Local Banking Laws

Although many international financial centers have branches or subsidiaries of well-known international banks, these banks are staffed by local nationals and their operations are subject to local laws and rules, which are often very different from those of the parent bank's jurisdiction.

Investor Protection

When selecting from a large number of locally incorporated, privately owned banks, you should closely examine each for stability. In the event of failure, the bank may not have a wealthy parent to support it. Most international financial centers have investor protection programs, but these may be limited by local regulations and should therefore be reviewed closely. For example, in the United Kingdom investors are only covered for deposits made in the local currency.

International Finance Experience

The offshore bank's experience with multicurrency and cross-border finance should also be investigated. Are letters of credit and similar documents everyday business for the bank, or does the bank provide more traditional local banking facilities?

Bank Autonomy and Authority

Branches of international banks should be scrutinized

for how much autonomy and on-site management they enjoy. Do they maintain all the accounts at their branch or keep them at some distant international branch in another jurisdiction? Are international transfers introduced and received directly or must they go through some central clearing process in another jurisdiction?

Also important is how much authority the local manager has to grant guarantees, accept letters of credit and conduct other international monetary transactions. Failure to obtain answers to these questions before a new account is opened can result in costly and frustrating delays.

Documentation and Signatory Requirements

The initial documentation required to open a foreign corporate account varies widely from bank to bank and country to country. The bank may require that documents:

- be officially translated;
- bear the company seal and all directors' signatures;
- be notarized; and/or
- be legalized by consular authentication or by an apostille affixed as provided under the Hague Convention.

The bank may further require:
- a certificate of good standing obtained from the jurisdictional government in which the company is incorporated confirming corporate existence;
- a legal opinion from an attorney licensed in the incorporating jurisdiction to confirm that the company has the legal capacity to open a bank account and to undertake the proposed transaction;
- references on the proposed signatories to a new account, which may entail direct contact

59

between the bankers in addition to written references; and/or

- details on the beneficial owner of the company, even in jurisdictions with no legal requirement for such information. Each piece of information provided raises the question of to whom else and under what circumstances might that information be available in the future?

If the bank lacks experience with the jurisdiction, its legal department may delay their acceptance of some or all of these prerequisites to opening an account.

Communications

Dealing with bankers at a distance necessitates that the bank accept instruction by fax. Surprisingly, some international banks will not accept instruction by fax or telephone. Those that do will insist on an indemnity signed by the directors of the company.

Language

When the account is finally opened, more difficulties may lie ahead. The variety of statements issued by banks around the world is tribute to man's inventiveness, but understanding what these papers actually say is another matter. Even if correspondence with the bank is in English throughout the account opening procedure, statements are often printed in the native language. Unless you know French, German, or Dutch, it is difficult to tell the debits from the credits. The charges are another problem altogether!

Currency

To many offshore centers, the dollar and pound sterling are foreign currency. The sale of dollars for deutsche marks, for example, attracts two lots of exchange commissions as the funds pass through the domestic currency on their way to another.

Many offshore banks offer currency checkbooks, but unless those checks are cleared through New York (if in dollars) or London (if in sterling), six weeks may pass before the recipient bank obtains cleared funds. The Eurocheque is sometimes a solution, which can be written for an agreed limit in any European currency. The recipient will enjoy cleared funds within a few days. Unfortunately, European banks are inclined to forget to tell prospective customers of this service.

Anyone attempting to open an offshore corporate account for the first time may think the bank is presenting every possible obstacle to opening a new account. Around the world, companies gather dust on shelves of lawyers' offices simply because attempts to open a foreign bank account proved too formidable for both attorney and client!

Nonetheless, such stringent requirements appear to be symptomatic of the times and actually offer investors additional security. In these days of highly publicized fraud and money laundering cases, banks need to be extremely cautious about whom they accept as a customer. Further, reputable offshore financial centers have regulatory authorities who insist that those operating in and from their territory follow the principle of "know your customer." The situation, however, should be looked at in perspective.

New accounts are opened in offshore centers on a daily basis and millions of legitimate dollars flow through them annually, all without the slightest problem. After all, international finance is the lifeblood of these centers. They have no other source of income, and they need the business!

Daily administration of the offshore company, if provided by professional corporate managers or a fiduciary, resolves many of the typical concerns cited above. A good administrator will know the precise requirements of each bank and the most efficient way to fulfill them. In turn, the banks will know from past experience that all accounts opened and operated by that administrator are well-managed, monitored, and maintained. The benefits of this good relationship are passed on to the client.

No bank can be all things to all people. Consequently, a good administrator will learn exactly what your banking needs are and match them to the most suitable offshore bank.

7 The Limited Liability Company

The limited liability company (also called the LLC) is a business entity just now becoming popular in the United States, although it's been available in Germany, France, and many other countries for decades. Until its recent acceptance by a number of states, the business executive had three common choices when forming a business: the sole proprietorship, the corporation, or the partnership.

The LLC is a hybrid between the partnership and the corporation. It has all the flexibility of a partnership to define its own management structure, rules of procedure, voting rights, distribution of profits, and myriad other details. The structure is created by a contract among all the parties. At the same time, if structured properly, all the members and the management enjoy the limited liability typical of a corporation.

It is generally assumed that the combination of these two elements is the reason most LLCs are formed, although there is a great deal of latitude with regard to the structure. It offers many advantages over the Subchapter S corporation, which has been the traditional method of combining corporate liability protection with partnership-type taxation.

HISTORY OF THE LLC

The origin of the modern LLC laws allowing limited liability companies is the German law of 1892, which created the GmbH (Gesellschaft mit beschranker Haftung). In the 60 years that followed, almost 20 countries adopted similar laws. In France, for example, the same type of company is known as the SARL (Societes de Responsabilite Limitee). In Central and South America it is known as the "limitada."

In the United States, the first state to adopt a modern limited liability company statute was Wyoming on March 4, 1977. Florida followed in 1982 by enacting a similar statute. Now a number of states have either enacted similar laws or have pending legislation. It has become the most talked about and most imitated new business law in America. However, the IRS gave no assurance that such an entity could qualify to be treated as a partnership until September 2, 1988, when Revenue Ruling 88-76 was issued. It was the first Revenue Ruling from the IRS regarding LLCs. In February 1993, the IRS issued four Revenue Rulings that describe the classification standards the IRS applies to LLCs that desire partnership tax treatment.

Now that the issue of pass-through tax treatment has been settled, it is time for business owners to seriously consider this form of entity when forming new ventures and to replace the form they previously adopted for existing enterprises. Some lawyers predict that the LLC will steadily gain popularity as people become educated about its benefits until it largely replaces the partnership and corporation as the preferred entity. Most states either have laws pending or a legislative committee studying the matter, so you should check on recent developments in your state.

Whether or not your state has an LLC law, if you are forming an investment or holding company not doing an active business, then you could use another state to form the LLC. Delaware is one of the best choices for forming an investment or holding company LLC. This arrangement also has the advantage of putting the legal entity in a state other than your own.

The Delaware LLC law was passed on October 1, 1992. Delaware has a long history as the home of the best corporate law in the United States. The law is considered to be promanagement and has a tradition of respecting good-faith management decisions. A strong partnership exists in Delaware between the corporate bar, the legislature, and the judiciary, which helps to maintain a legal atmosphere second to none. This tradition of excellence in corporate law is likely to attract those who want to form LLCs in the United States.

The Delaware LLC statute is clearly the most flexible. It follows a tradition that Delaware lawyers call the "freedom of contract," which allows broad flexibility among members of an LLC to create the details of the structure of the company in ways that best suit their needs. More than any other state LLC statute, the Delaware law allows the parties to draft the LLC company agreement as they require and "opt in" the elements they desire without a lot of regulations or restrictions.

The Delaware law presumes that the entity will be treated as a partnership unless otherwise classified and provides extensive protection to members and managers. It does not require that the duration be stated in the certificate of formation, and it limits the liability of the members to their investment in the company. The Delaware law also allows for a structure in which the death of a member will not cause an automatic dissolution. All these elements together are not included in the Wyoming statute or in any of the others. The drafters of the Delaware LLC law sought deliberately to create it in such a way as to give maximum flexibility, thus allowing creativity among the drafters of the company agreements. Delaware LLCs pay an annual state fee of $100, the same as limited partnerships.

Legislation was passed in July 1993 that allows Delaware corporations to convert their status to LLC by merging the old corporation into a new LLC. The new LLC may take the same name as the corporation with proper filing details.

Delaware has again distinguished itself, and it promises to be one of the leaders in the formation and maintenance of LLCs.

COMPARISON WITH THE SUBCHAPTER S CORPORATION

An LLC provides its members with liability protection and tax treatment similar to that enjoyed by stockholders of an S corporation. However, an S corporation is subject to the following statutory restrictions:

1) It is limited to one class of ownership interests (i.e., one class of stock).
2) It must be a domestic corporation.
3) It may not have more than 35 stockholders.
4) Stockholders may not include other corporations, nonresident aliens, partnerships, certain trusts, pension funds, or charitable organizations.
5) It cannot have subsidiaries.

None of these restrictions applies to the LLC. This flexibility creates considerable freedom in planning distributions and special allocations of income and loss.

COMPARISON WITH THE LIMITED PARTNERSHIP

An LLC is taxed in basically the same manner as a limited partnership without the following disadvantages that limited partnerships have with regard to liability:

1) A limited partnership must have at least one general partner who is liable for the debts of the partnership, while all of the members of an LLC may be protected from such liability.

2) The participation of limited partners in the management of a limited partnership can result in a loss of limited liability protection, while such participation by members of an LLC will not have this effect provided such management does not violate the applicable LLC statute. Accordingly, a member of an LLC that is treated as a limited partnership would be able to "materially participate" for purposes of Section 469 of the U.S. Internal Revenue Code, which limits the utilization of passive activity losses and credits while maintaining limited liability protection.

FOR WHICH PURPOSES ARE LLCs CURRENTLY BEING FORMED?

Venture Capital, Real Estate, and Other Investment Firms

Control, division of profits and losses, and many other aspects may be specified in the agreement, plus pass-through tax treatment when properly structured.

Family Business Enterprises

Control can be spelled out and estate planning considerations can be customized as an integral part of the agreement. Pass-through tax treatment when properly structured.

Entrepreneurial Start-Ups

Pass-through tax treatment like Subchapter S but without the restrictions on ownership, if properly structured. No limit on the number of investors.

Professional Corporations

Accountants, attorneys, doctors, psychologists, financial planners, and all professionals now working through partnerships can free themselves of the liability for their partners' actions while retaining the same control structure as their partnership.

THE FORMATION PROCESS

Each party in an LLC must agree to a contract with all the other members that will become the "constitution" of the company. This document may be called the Company Agreement, Articles of Organization, Minutes of the First Meeting of Members, or any other name unless the particular state has a required name.

This agreement should set forth the company's policy and procedure regarding important matters such as voting rights and restrictions, differences among members or classes of members, investment into the company by each member, restrictions on access to information among members, rights of management, restrictions on transfer of ownership interests, distribution of profits, required meetings (if any), notices of meetings, quorum rules, inclusion of new members, continuation options upon the death of a member, and all other provisions the company wants to include.

Most states allow the inclusion of provisions and elements almost without restriction. This gives the drafters of the agreement the opportunity to be creative. Since this form of entity is relatively new, all the available inclusions will not be commonly known immediately. This represents a danger to the LLC, as it can only change its agreement when it has the unanimous agreement of its members.

In drafting the agreement, careful consideration must be given to the IRS's position regarding tax classification of the entity. Although the law allows tremen-

68

dous flexibility, the IRS is very specific
applies when determining whether to
partnership or as a corporation. Sinc
treatment is expected to be a prim
most organizers, the drafters must create a
that provides for IRS rules. (If your lawyer or acc
is not familiar with these rules, they are contained in *CFR* 301.7701-2, 3, and 4. This is legalese for Section 301
of Title 28 of the *Code of Federal Regulations*.)

Although do-it-yourself incorporation is generally
not a problem, because the limited liability company
agreement is as complex as a partnership and calls for
originality and creativity, it is probably best to use a
lawyer experienced in such matters. (He does not neces-
sarily have to be a lawyer in the state where it is
formed—you may find better experience elsewhere, and
that experience will usually translate to the state that
has just enacted a statute more readily than a local
lawyer will absorb the nuances of a strange entity.) The
differences and possibilities are too vast for a simple do-
it-yourself procedure to be wise at this time.

WHO SHOULD NOT FORM AN LLC?

- Companies planning to operate their business
  in a state that does not currently recognize
  LLCs should seriously consider the consequences of losing their limitation on liability
  in that state before forming an LLC.
- Entrepreneurs who do not want to bear the
  responsibility, cost, and possible future con-
  straints of a customized company structure
  should consider sticking to the time-tested and
  more rigid structure that a general stock corporation offers.
- Sole owner companies cannot be LLCs. An LLC
  must have two members, by definition, or it

automatically dissolves. (Of course, the second owner could be a children's trust or a family limited partnership holding 1 percent.)

GETTING STARTED

For more information on forming a Delaware LLC, write to LLC Information Package, 818 Washington Street, Wilmington, DE, 19801. Delaware has traditionally been one of the best states in which to register companies and hold assets because the court system is very protective of private property.

If you already have either a regular corporation or an S corporation, you will definitely want to consider the advantages of using an LLC. By replacing your S corporation with an LLC, you avoid the risk of the IRS suddenly deciding to tax the S corporation at regular corporate rates because you made some small mistake that caused the S corporation election to be revoked.

Another little known tax angle is using an LLC along with your regular corporation. For example, suppose you have a business that owns its own building. You can use a regular corporation for the active business and take advantage of the tax breaks available to corporations, such as being able to set up a pension plan and get health insurance.

You then have the LLC own the building and rent it to the business corporation. The business pays rent to the LLC, which becomes taxable income to you, but since this is rent income, not salary from the business, you don't have to pay social security tax on it. And having the building owned by the LLC still gives you limited liability to protect you against lawsuits that might arise from being a property owner.

8 Limited Partnerships: An Authentic Judgment-Proofing Device

If properly directed toward the goal of asset protection, a limited partnership, particularly a "family partnership" (one of the best known variations) can greatly reduce federal and state income and inheritance taxes and provide maximum personal insulation from lawsuits and other potential liabilities.

Used successfully in the United States for almost two centuries, the continuing popularity of the limited partnership among knowledgeable financial planners attests to its effectiveness in protecting assets, but only if properly organized and operated as the law requires.

GENERAL PARTNERSHIPS

One of the earlier definitions of a partnership still quoted in court cases today was provided by Chancellor James Kent of the New York appellate courts in 1840. He described a partnership as "a contract between two or more competent persons to place their money, effects, labor and skill, and some or all of them, in lawful commerce or business, and to divide the profit and bear the loss in certain proportions."

In the broadest sense, a "general partnership," as it is

called, is an association of two or more persons (or other legal entities) formed to conduct a business for mutual profit. More than 90 percent of all partnerships in the United States are general partnerships, businesses governed by the Uniform Partnership Act, which is now law in 47 of the 50 states. (Alabama, Louisiana, and Maine follow common law principles of partnership law or have their own specialized statutes.)

In general partnerships, each partner is a co-owner jointly running the business with the objective of a profit, and each acts as an agent for, and has a fiduciary relationship with, the other partners. As a result, each partner is personally liable for the acts of the other partners, including partnership debts and liabilities. By their common agreement the partners may have the same or differing capital investments and may share profits and losses in the same or varying proportions, usually corresponding to each one's original investment.

A partnership is recognized by the law for most purposes, including making contracts, obtaining credit, filing bankruptcy, incurring debt, marshaling assets, and acquiring and transferring property. But a partnership, as such, does not pay tax—its partners do as individuals owing income tax on their partnership income. Section 761 of the U.S. Internal Revenue Code echoes this broad description by referring to a partnership as "a syndicate, group, pool, joint venture, or other unincorporated organization through or by means of which any business, financial operation or venture is carried on."

Some Real Disadvantages

From the standpoint of asset protection, general partnerships (as compared to limited partnerships discussed below) present the possibility of major problems and pitfalls.

Each general partner can be held personally liable for all partnership debts or liabilities resulting from another partner's or an agent's negligent or harmful acts. General partnerships often must be dissolved when one partner files personal bankruptcy or dies, unless immediate arrangements are made for a buyout of that partner's interest, or unless the partnership agreement anticipates such events and makes contingent continuation provisions. Usually a deceased general partner's interest is subjected to estate probate, which is often a lengthy and cumbersome process, and estate and inheritance taxes are levied on the value of that interest, diminishing what goes to the heirs.

General partnerships are also often faced with the usual personal problems inherent in any joint ownership arrangement: sudden death, divorce, or inheritance of the partnership share by nonmembers who may be undesirable as partners. Considering all the uncontrollable variables of a general partnership, you can understand why this legal device may be successful in allowing associates to conduct a joint business enterprise but is decidedly less than useful in personal asset protection. In fact, it could complicate things considerably when the objective is asset protection.

LIMITED PARTNERSHIPS

A "limited partnership" must be composed of at least one general partner (who is usually the managing partner) and one or more "limited partners," also called "special partners." The limited partner, who must take no part in the day-to-day management, has no personal liability beyond the amount of his or her agreed cash or other capital investment in the partnership. The limited partner does have a right to receive agreed amounts of partnership income when it is distributed. This arrangement is accomplished by specific written provisions in the "partnership agreement," the basic document governing the partnership.

The concept of general partnerships was well established in English common law, but limited partnerships are an American invention. Limited partnership arrangements were first recognized in the United States in New York statutory law in 1822. By 1916, the National Conference of Commissioners on Uniform Laws had approved the first Model Uniform Limited Partnership Act largely based on the French Civil Code, which permitted similar business arrangements. Today all states have adopted the Uniform Limited Partnership Act with some variations except Alabama, Connecticut, Kansas, Kentucky, Louisiana, Maine, Mississippi, Oregon, and Wyoming.

In states where it has become law, the Uniform Limited Partnership Act sets the rights and responsibilities of the limited and general partners among themselves and with other people with whom they have business dealings. The major features of this law are, first, protect the limited partner from liability as a general partner (unless he or she actually takes an active part in control of the business); second, give the limited partner full right and access to all partnership information; and third, guarantee the limited partner his or her share of profits or other compensation by way of regular income payments.

Protection Against Creditors

Perhaps one of the greatest advantages afforded by a limited partnership is that a personal creditor of a limited partner usually cannot attach that partner's interest in the partnership. A personal creditor can only obtain what is known as a "charging order" (more about this later), a relatively unattractive remedy in the judgment collection process usually requiring the creditor to wait for some future distribution of partnership income to the debtor/partner, which is a totally discretionary act within the power of the managing partner. In other words, a creditor could wait forever.

The courts of the state of California, which has one of

the most liberal partnership laws, have recently called into question the near personal-creditor-proof status of a limited partner's partnership assets. In several cases the California courts held that, under certain equitable circumstances, a debtor's limited partnership interest can be foreclosed to honor a personal judgment against him or her—a major departure from past holdings and a significant lessening of limited partnership asset protection, at least in California. The reasoning behind such decisions seems to be that in some cases, limited partnerships are found to be not actual operating businesses but simply legal shams designed to protect assets. It remains to be seen whether other states will follow what is still a novel, if disturbing, trend in this area of the law.

Questions about validity do not usually arise when a partnership is formed in which capital is a major income-producing factor, and each partner contributes his or her own share of that capital, or even when the partner's capital share is a gift, as to a minor as a partner, which the law allows. Warning flags are raised, especially by the IRS, when the enterprise is a service business, and a partner whose interest is acquired by gift (especially a minor) contributes little in the way of services. In such cases the IRS is likely to contest the partnership status of that partner.

Formation of a Limited Partnership
The Uniform Limited Partnership Act outlines the general procedure to be followed in establishing a limited partnership.

Many state statutes require a formal procedure for the formation and registration of a limited partnership, and good faith compliance is necessary. As notice and protection to the public, the law often requires the formal public registration of partnership agreements and the filing of a "certificate of affirmation" or a formal "articles of a limited partnership" signed and registered with a state agency or with the county clerk as notice of the business's scope and the limits of each partner's liability. In many states, failure to file such registration statements, including the names and addresses of the partners, can be prosecuted as a crime. False statements made in a limited partnership registration may even negate the limited personal liability of any partner who has knowledge of the false statement.

In spite of all these technical requirements, a common law general partnership can be established by oral or written agreement of the parties or even reasonably implied in law (a so-called partnership by estoppel), as when a third party extends credit to two or more businessmen assumed to be partners because of their conduct over a period of time.

Usually the law forbids the public use of the name of a limited partner as part of the partnership name (unless it is the same family name of the managing or other general partner) so that a false reliance will not be created in the public mind concerning that limited partner's liability. It is a basic legal requirement that in order to preserve his or her limited liability, a limited partner cannot take any active role in the actual management of the partnership.

The Partnership Agreement

The rules of law that are generally applicable to the formation of contracts apply to a partnership agreement.

There must be "valid consideration" (something of value must be paid or pledged); individual legal capacity to enter into a contract; and informed consent—but the essential distinguishing feature of a partnership is an agreement to conduct a joint business for the mutual profit of the partners.

The Revised Uniform Limited Partnership Act, an updated version of the earlier 1916 model law, which has been adopted in a few states, repeats the original definition of a limited partnership as being formed by two or more persons under the laws of a state and having one or more general partners and one or more limited partners. The new Uniform Act more fully defines "person" as a natural person, some other partnership or limited partnership (domestic or foreign), a trust, an estate, an association, or a corporation. As you can see, the legal (and tax) consequences of bringing together such parties within the scope of one limited partnership is nearly endless and often very beneficial for asset protection. But again, only if it is done correctly.

Although a limited or any partnership agreement can be informal, as indicated above, obviously it is far better to set down the exact terms in writing. This provides the best protection for the partners themselves. These documents, although they are in many respects the most important part of the partnership, are technical in nature and usually require legal and tax counsel to ensure both the partners' maximum advantage and the validity of the agreement.

Among other things, limited partnership agreements normally describe such matters as:

1) the cash, property, or services each partner will contribute at the beginning and at later dates and the extent of obligation of later contributions upon request;
2) whether the partnership is to be in perpetuity; or, in the alternative, the termination date; or a description of events that will cause an earlier end to the partnership, such as death of a party, change in tax advantages, unprofitable business conditions, or majority vote;
3) the name, purpose, and principal place of business and the location of the books and records and responsibility for their maintenance;
4) each general partner's rights and responsibili-

ties concerning management, including voting rights, full-time duties, and noncompetition restrictions on a partner's other business activities;
5) stated percentages of profits and losses for each partner and by what method, and under what circumstances, these figures may change;
6) provisions for the withdrawal of partners, the admission of new partners, and the method of asset distribution upon termination or dissolution. If the agreement is silent on asset distribution, the Uniform Act provides a method;
7) an optional provision that the capital of a deceased partner shall remain in the business requiring surviving partners to pay interest, or a share of the profits, or ultimately return the deceased partner's share to his or her heirs, or reach a settlement with the executor of the deceased's estate as to eventual repayment.

The Managing General Partner

The Uniform Limited Partnership Act requires that there be at least one general partner who actually manages the business.

This general partner, by the terms of the agreement, may be given complete or shared management control with another general partner, but each general partner is fully personally liable as such for the partnership debts and liabilities. It is not uncommon for the managing general partner to be empowered to decide about the needs for additional working capital to expand the business or whether or not profits are to be withheld from limited partners and used instead for future development.

Because the success of a limited partnership depends so much on the management abilities of the person or persons who serve as managing general partner, such agreements often provide that upon a general partner's death,

78

bankruptcy, transfer of his or her interest while still alive, or legal incompetence, the partnership will dissolve unless all the partners agree to its continuation.

For a general managing partner, even one who holds a small portion (say 5 percent) of the partnership assets, his or her status confers near total control over the entire business enterprise—which may be worth many millions of dollars. Thus a spouse who serves as a general partner, with his or her spouse and heirs as limited partners, can limit estate and inheritance taxes, which at his death will be levied only on the value of his small interest, even though during his life he controls the assets worth many times his share.

A general partner does share in all profits, and since partnerships are not taxed as such, he or she can avoid the double taxation imposed on corporations (the tax on corporate profits plus individual income taxes on corporate officers' salaries and shareholders' dividends). A general partner has the ability to withdraw his or her full contribution without taxation; jointly manage and conduct the business, along with other general partners, with complete access to all books and financial information; and obtain joint credit with other partners.

FAMILY LIMITED PARTNERSHIPS

The legal relationship popularly known as a family partnership is usually created as a vehicle to transfer income and assets from the owner/organizer of a business, or anyone who accumulates valuable assets or is in a high income tax bracket, to members of his or her own family so as to limit everyone's personal and tax liability to the maximum extent possible.

A family partnership is really nothing more than a limited partnership in which family members, rather than nonfamily business associates, are the limited partners usually with a parent or grandparent as the managing general partner. Of course, this arrangement comes with the potential for all the usual arguments for which families are notorious as well as the great advantages close relationships make possible.

It is understandable that a legal arrangement built on family economic interests is popular in the United States, where much of the country's wealth is held in millions of family businesses. One estimate holds that family businesses account for more than half the gross domestic product and provide about half of the nation's jobs. Oddly enough, only 3 out of 10 family businesses survive into the second generation and 1 in 10 lasts to the third generation. The average family enterprise lasts only about 24 years. Many of the reasons for the demise of family businesses are found in human dynamics, which overlap the problems of both family and business, either of which can be daunting on their own. Active family partnerships often mirror all these concerns and cease because of them.

Unlike a family corporation, which many use to protect assets, a family limited partnership offers the advantages of an agreement allowing the parties great precision in defining their rights and allows withdrawal of property with far fewer tax problems.

Under the U.S. Internal Revenue Code, the "family" of an individual (and therefore a possible family limited partnership) can include his or her spouse, ancestors, lineal descendants, and any trust established for the primary benefit of such persons. "Ancestors" include grandparents, but not in-laws, aunts, uncles, great-aunts, or great-uncles. "Lineal descendants" include children, grandchildren, and great-grandchildren, but exclude sons-in-law and daughters-in-law and nieces and nephews.

In *Culbertson v. United States*, 337 U.S. 733 (1949), the Supreme Court upheld family partnerships even if they included only a husband, wife, and their children, the deciding factor being whether the "partners really and truly intended to join together and share in the profits and losses for both."

The U.S. Internal Revenue Code confirms a person's right to transfer an interest in a partnership to a member of his or her family either by gift or purchase. If it is a personal service business, the donee-partner must take an active part in the business, which makes this type of partnership unsuitable for estate planning, at least if the donee is a minor.

In order to protect a family limited partnership from possible legal challenge, there should be a formal written agreement that spells out the limits and powers of each partner and a complete record of all filings and transactions. The managing partner should be paid reasonable compensation, and transfers to the donee partners, especially minors, should not be in the form of discharging normal parental obligations like medical care and educational support. Trustees for minors should be completely independent, not in any way subject to the donee's control. Title to assets should be formally transferred to the family partnership so that it becomes the true owner of record.

Any restrictions on a limited partner that diminish their control over their own partnership interest can make the arrangement vulnerable to IRS attack, including requirements that the interest be left in the business for a long period of years or limiting the partner's power over distributions of income and giving such power instead to the managing partner/donee.

In order to recognize a minor as a limited partner, courts will almost always require the appointment of a fiduciary trustee with complete powers to manage the minor limited partner's interest. The only exception occurs in the exceedingly rare instance when a minor has sufficient maturity and ability to act on his own as a limited partner.

Advantages and Disadvantages

For a person wishing to make large asset gifts, family partnerships have several advantages:

- The arrangements are simple, needing only an agreement, a deed of gift, and a certificate of family limited partnership. Property need be transferred only once—to the partnership—and later changes of donor and donee interests require only amendments to the partnership documents. The only public records involved are deeds to real estate transfers and registration of the partnership itself, if state law requires this.
- It eliminates the need for ancillary probates of real property located in states other than that of the donee's residence when such property is deeded to the partnership. Most states exempt such partnership property from probate.
- The donor of property retains a great measure of personal control over that property, especially when he or she is the managing general partner or sole general partner.
- Since a partnership is not a taxable entity, making gifts of family partnerships avoids the double taxation to which net income is subjected in an ordinary family corporation.

The only real disadvantage of the family limited partnership—and one that proper planning can avoid—is the possible successful challenge to the partnership status by the IRS or a partner's personal judgment creditor. In such cases, courts look more closely at these family partnerships to make sure arms-length dealing and fairness does occur.

I mentioned successful creditor attacks in some

California cases, but there are also special IRS income tax requirements that must be met. The partnership must include capital income producing as a material factor in its activities, and the donee must become the real owner of the interest in that capital. Otherwise, partnership income will be taxed to the donor alone, depriving the donor of any income-shifting tax advantages. Where such issues may exist, the IRS is usually willing to fight.

In summary, if it is done right, the family limited partnership is a good device for income shifting, good for the conduct of a family business where the corporate form presents tax problems, good for maintaining control of assets while passing them on to others, good for estate planning, and good for insulation from creditors' attacks.

Threats to Limited Liability

Family limited partnerships have been under legal siege both in federal and state courts, usually on the grounds that the entity is in fact a sham—not really an operating business, but a means of avoiding taxes, creditors, or other liabilities.

If judicial acceptance grows for the views expressed in the recent California cases holding a limited partner's partnership interest liable for personal debts, it could have a serious impact on family partnerships as asset protection vehicles. This threat makes it all the more imperative that family partnerships (or any limited partnerships) meet all the required legal criteria, both when they are first established and in later operation. To conduct the affairs of the partnership in a way that threatens the protected liability status of limited partners is to defeat the very purpose for which it was created.

One of the principal justifications for laws allowing limited partnership protection is to prevent creditors of one partner from disrupting partnership business continuity—and harming the other partners by such a foreclosure. Although a partnership is usually thought to operate a commercial business enterprise, it can also be used to control personal assets such as a home or other real estate, personal property, and intangibles such as stocks, bonds, and even insurance. However, if a limited partnership's only business purpose is to hold title to a family's assets, including its personal residence, against a personal creditor's suit, it may be difficult to sustain an argument in court that the family partnership has any real commercial business that deserves protection. Certainly, allowing a personal creditor to foreclose on a partnership interest in such a case would not disrupt any general commercial enterprise, nor would any innocent, nonrelated third parties be prejudiced.

In a series of court cases in recent years (some appealed to the U.S. Supreme Court) the IRS has successfully challenged the claimed validity of both limited and family partnerships. In considering such challenges, the courts have imposed a series of tests that must be met in order to create a legally viable family (or any limited) partnership. Among other factors in its examination, the court will inquire:

- Whether each partner (especially a minor) has true title to and control of his or her interest;
- What was and is the true intent and relationship of the parties, regardless of the statements in the partnership articles;
- What capital and/or skill each partner actually did and does contribute; and
- Whether each limited partner really controls the income paid to him and its disposition.

These tests mean that a family partnership in a service business, like any limited partnership, must have partners who actually perform important work on a continuing basis and/or partners who really contribute

84

capital or assets of some tangible kind. The law does allow a limited partner to receive his or her partnership interest as a gift, but if the recipient is a minor, someone other than the donor of the gift must serve as legal custodian of that minor's interest until he or she reaches majority, 18 years old in most states, or there is a risk that a court will declare the arrangement to be void.

A limited partner may also purchase his or her partnership interest with payment out of future partnership profits. But there are restrictions on giving and purchasing limited partnership interests, and a court will scrutinize whether the donor actually relinquishes control and ownership of the interest before truly giving it over to the donee or purchaser.

MORE THAN ONE MAY BE NEEDED

If a large amount of money is involved in the enterprise, it is better to create more than one limited partnership. One can hold liquid assets such as cash, securities, bonds, certificates of deposit, precious metals, life insurance policies, and negotiable instruments. The other can hold title to assets, such as real estate and business property, which might be more vulnerable to creditor attack and attachment.

As in any limited partnership, the managing general partner exercises control over all family partnership assets. Limited partners who are also family members cannot and must not assert any power in management, or they will jeopardize their own protected status.

With the caveats expressed concerning recent court decisions, family partnership assets are still generally safe from the personal creditors of limited partners. This safety is improved by using a family partnership as part of an overall plan, which is properly prepared by professionals and not as a do-it-yourself entity in isolation. Additional safety can be achieved by using a Delaware partnership for liquid assets such as insurance policies and brokerage accounts, since Delaware is a state that is very protective of private property.

A partnership's creditors can only attack a limited partner's interest to the extent of that partner's actual capital investment, and then only with extreme procedural difficulty and usually little productive result. For example, a partnership can accumulate its assets as it sees fit, but it cannot be compelled to distribute them to the partners, thus protecting both those assets and the partners from a creditor's charging order seeking to attach such assets.

There is no legal bar to a parent/managing partner's contributing the majority of the family partnership's assets over a period of years in annual gifts or receiving in return only a small percentage of ownership interest. Once this transfer is made to the partnership, the arrangement gives the donor's creditors very little to pursue. Such gifts should never be made with creditors breathing down the donor's neck but should be planned well in advance to avoid any trouble.

Similarly, when income is distributed in a family or any limited partnership, the distribution does not have to be in proportion to a partner's exact investment or degree of ownership. Payments can be in any proportion and selected family members can be given a disproportionately large share. Whatever the income distribution may be, each recipient partner is liable for U.S. income taxes as ordinary income at the time of the distribution.

Keep in mind also that any legal entity can be a general or limited partner, including a domestic or foreign trust, a corporation, an estate, the custodian of a minor, or an association. This flexibility for a partner's legal form allows a managing general partner of a limited or family partnership to incorporate for that management purpose, providing the manager still greater personal protection from creditors and possibly a lower tax rate. It also allows for the transfer of assets to a limited partner, which may be a foreign asset trust—a possible double wall of asset protection potential creditors will have to breach.

THE LIMITED PARTNER

In order for a limited partner to effect and maintain his or her limited liability:

1) the limited partnership must be created in good faith compliance with all statutes;
2) a limited partner's surname cannot be used in the business; and
3) a limited partner can take no part in the conduct of the business.

A limited partner cannot assign, sell, or mortgage his or her interest in any specific partnership property, because to do so would destroy the voluntary nature of the partnership association and, in effect, force a new partner on the others without their consent. But a limited partner can assign, sell, or mortgage his or her property interest to another partner, assuming the articles of partnership do not forbid this. In addition, any false statements made on the registration form, which are known to a limited partner and on which third parties rely, may destroy limited liability.

A limited partner's interest in specific partnership property (the title to which he or she holds jointly with the other partners in what the law calls a "tenancy in partnership") cannot be subjected to garnishment, attachment, or execution by a judgment creditor of that partner. First claim on partnership assets rests with creditors of the partnership itself.

However, each partner also has a valuable interest in the partnership, which the Uniform Act defines as the share of profits and surplus, after the partnership debts are paid, accounts are settled, and rights of the individual partners are adjusted according to their articles of agreement. This remaining interest is treated as personal property under the Uniform Act and is assignable. Such assignment does not in any way impair the partnership itself, and the assignee of such interest obtains no right to participate in management.

In theory, a personal judgment creditor of a limited partner has a claim against the value of the partner's undivided partnership interest. In fact that interest is neither tangible nor capable of definition until the perhaps distant day comes when the partnership dissolves, business ends, all partnership debts have been fully satisfied, and the pro rata share of each partner has been calculated.

These rules effectively bar attachment, execution, and garnishment of all property held jointly in a tenancy in partnership, as well as strictly curtail a personal creditor's ability to reach a partner's interest in the partnership itself. However, a personal creditor is not without some remedies.

CHARGING ORDERS: BETTER THAN NOTHING?

In a few jurisdictions, including Arkansas, Connecticut, Georgia, New York, Ohio, Pennsylvania, and Texas, courts have held that the undivided interest of a partner in his or her partnership business, once determined, is subject to levy in the same manner as other property.

The Uniform Partnership Act provides that a judgment creditor (or in some states, any creditor) of a limited partner may obtain a court order "charging" that partner's interest in the partnership with future payment of an obligation, including interest.

The charging order has the character of a lien against that partner's interest, but it gives the personal creditor no priority over partnership creditors. The court may appoint a receiver entitled to receive the partner's share of profits or other money due and also may grant the receiver power to seek protection to conserve property or take other action, such as seek to void fraudulent conveyances. An energetic judgment creditor can even seek to foreclose the limited partner's interest in the firm and purchase it at sale, but once that is done he has nothing more than he had before except direct ownership of the interest and lots of lawyer's bills. At that point, the creditor could seek judicial dissolution of the firm and a final distribution of the assets—something few courts would be willing to grant in the absence of iron-clad proof of special circumstances, such as conspiracy and fraud on the part of all partners. None but the last of these judicial activities impairs the limited partner's continued status as a partner.

From the selfish point of view of a limited partner/debtor all this means is that his or her partnership interest, which can be of enormous value, is effectively shielded from all but the most determined and deep-pocketed creditors. From the vantage point of a family limited partnership, it could be an excellent device to protect assets but only if it is properly implemented and managed with professional assistance and thus is immune to legal challenge.

A GOOD JUDGMENT-PROOFING IDEA

From the foregoing you should properly conclude that a family limited partnership has great potential as a shelter from creditors for both personal and family business assets, and it can certainly help to reduce estate and inheritance taxes. Income taxes can also be reduced substantially as family partnership income is spread among all partner/family members, including younger members with less income, meaning a lower overall family income tax rate.

But limited partnerships, family-based or otherwise, come at a price. You must be exceedingly careful to comply with all local and state laws and regulations governing registration, firm names, and use of fictitious business names. Separate partnership bank accounts must be established with legal control of the funds clearly indicated. If a donee is to be a limited partner, his or her partnership interest must be reflected in all insurance policies, deeds, leases, business contracts, and any litigation that might occur. All statutory documentary requirements must be scrupulously met and complete financial records maintained on an annual basis. Tax returns must be filed. Most importantly, when donee interests are involved, the donor must fully transfer to the donee all rights, titles, and interest in order to avoid tax or legal contests of the partnership status.

While there is flexibility in a family partnership, especially for the managing general partner, there are also restrictions. The donor of the partnership assets still must deed absolutely his or her assets to the partnership, and normally all of the partners must agree before partnership assets can be sold or transferred. As with any partnership, unless the partnership agreement specifically provides otherwise, one partner's death or bankruptcy may force the dissolution of the partnership (or a forced buyout) at an inopportune time for the sale and distribution of assets. Again, remember partnership income, dividends, and assets are taxed fully as part of a deceased partner's estate, are subject to inheritance taxes, and upon distribution as income may place a partner in a significantly higher personal income tax bracket at an unexpected time.

Unless carefully crafted by experienced legal experts, your partnership may be vulnerable to IRS officials or creditors eager to use legal loopholes to destroy your protection. That could mean that after you are gone and well after creating an ostensible family partnership, your family may find itself in a financial and asset situation far worse than if nothing had been done. But this form of asset ownership and business has been around for 200 years—the problems (and the ways around them) are well known and can be avoided. There are no shortcuts, but there are many possible rewards.

Establishing a family limited partnership obviously does not in itself guarantee either increased income or fully adequate asset protection benefits. The value of a family partnership, like any investment device, comes from proper initiation, continued good management, and many wise decisions. What the limited partnership does offer is an established tool, recognized in law, which can enable you to achieve your desired financial goals.

9 Legal Insurance: It Does Exist

How many times have you received shoddy merchandise or service for good money? How many times has someone bumped into your car, causing a few hundred dollars' damage? How many times has someone tried to take advantage of you, and you were unable to do anything about it because legal action, or even getting legal advice, would have been too expensive?

This is not a problem for rich people, who can call a lawyer whenever they want to. It is not even a problem for many poor people, who can get legal aid. It is a problem for average, hard working, middle-income Americans.

But there is a solution—legal protection plans.

Legal protection plans were introduced in Europe about 70 years ago and over the years have become very common and popular in Europe. As simple and as necessary as they are, legal protection plans have not become available in the United States until quite recently.

Statistics indicate the average American faces a greater risk of being in court than in the hospital. Annually millions of lawsuits are filed in the United States, and over one-third of the population experiences problems with legal ramifications. Unfortunately, most consumers in the greatest need of legal services do not seek help because they do not know how to select competent legal counsel and fear the cost of that counsel.

Pre-Paid Legal Services, Inc., formed in 1972, pioneered the legal plan industry in the United States. It is now a large public company listed on the American Stock Exchange. Their products are to attorney fees what prepaid medical plans are to doctor and hospital bills. The company offers plans that make services available through a national network of independent attorneys under contract with the company. In most states, services include unlimited telephone consultations, legal correspondence on your behalf, will preparation and maintenance, legal document review (to protect you before you sign), motor vehicle violation defense, vehicle damage recovery, trial defense in civil actions, and IRS audit protection. Depending on the state and the coverage selected, costs are in the range of $9.95 to $25 per month. For more information, write to PPLS Information, P.O. Box 540, Upper Marlboro, MD 20772.

Individuals who are interested in selling the Pre-Paid Legal Services plan may obtain information by sending $3.00 for the PPLS Information Package to Choyo Gomez, P.O. Box 1160, Pomona, CA, 91766.

10 The Trust as Asset Protector

WHAT IS A TRUST?

In its simplest definition, a trust is a legal device allowing title to and possession of property to be held, used, and/or managed by one person, the trustee, for the benefit of one or more other persons, the beneficiaries.

A trust is one of the most flexible legal mechanisms available in American law, and is useful for almost any purpose that is not illegal or against public policy. A trust can conduct a business; hold title to and invest in real estate, cash, stocks, bonds, negotiable instruments, and all sorts of personal property; take care of minors or the elderly; pay medical, educational, or other expenses; provide financial support in retirement, marriage, or divorce; assist in the execution of a premarital agreement; and serve as a major avenue of avoidance for the muddle of probate and the burden of inheritance taxes.

And in some carefully arranged circumstances, a trust can serve as an excellent asset protection device.

An Ancient Custom
Trusts are rooted in antiquity. Evidence of the earliest known trust was discovered in an Egyptian tomb—part

of a document containing a personal last will and testament written in the year 1805 B.C. There were trusts in both Roman and Greek law. The Romans called it *fiducia*, from which our word fiduciary is derived.

Roman law officially recognized the trust concept during the reign of the Roman Emperor Augustus Caesar nearly 2,000 years ago. This imperial acceptance of the trust resulted from the perfidious actions of a deceitful friend, who was asked by a wealthy Roman father to act as the trustee of his property in the event of his death. The father's wife was not a Roman citizen and because of this impediment, neither she nor their children could inherit his property under Roman law. The concerned father proposed to will his property to his friend in return for the friend's promise to use it only for the benefit of the children. After the father's death, the friend inherited the property but soon betrayed the trust, using the property for his own benefit instead.

This wrong came to the attention of the emperor, who ordered the trustee brought before the Roman courts. The judges found the friend guilty of a breach of trust, for which he was punished. The ruling was the first recorded judicial approval of the trust in Roman law, and afterward the device became so popular among Romans that a special court was created to deal exclusively with trust matters.

Ancient Germanic and French law had a trust concept, and from the time of Mohammed the concept of the trust was a fundamental principle of Islamic law. In the Middle Ages when the quasi-religious Order of Knights Templar acted as Paris-based international financiers, the trust was a common method used for royal and ecclesiastical investors who wished to shield their financial activity from the public and each other.

The trust was also probably the world's first tax shelter. In 16th-century England, trusts took on tax shelter aspects that allowed citizens to avoid feudal taxes on property inheritances and transfers.

Over the centuries, the concept of the trust was greatly refined through use and development, especially in British common law nations and the United States. American court decisions have also played a large role in refining the law of domestic trusts with significant legal and tax consequences.

TRUST TROUBLES IN AMERICA

In the recent past, the trust was promoted by investment advisors and lawyers (whose technical assistance became essential for trust creation) as perhaps the best method for wealthy people both to shield assets from potential attack and to guarantee the future use of property in the manner the owner intended after his or her demise.

Unfortunately, far too many investors blindly followed unsound advice about trusts. They or their heirs eventually found themselves enmeshed in turmoil produced by trust "plans" using prefabricated legal forms, which were held to be legally deficient and nullified by court and IRS decisions. Volumes of reported court cases attest to the sad fact that these bogus "trust experts" had been selling "foolproof" trust arrangements that were, in reality, little more than transparent tax and creditor avoidance schemes.

This unfortunate historic experience underscores the absolute necessity when creating a trust to choose an expert attorney who is thoroughly knowledgeable in trust and tax law, and who has the professional ability to tailor the trust to your exact needs and the demands of the IRS. Do otherwise and instead of protecting your assets, you could be added to the long list of the dispossessed spending costly years in court defending what remains of those assets—and yourself.

TRUST CREATION

The person who creates a trust (variously called the "donor," "grantor," or "settlor") conveys legal title to a body of his or her real or personal property or money (the "corpus") to a third party (the "trustee"), perhaps a trusted friend, professional financial manager, or a bank with a trust department, to be managed or invested by the trustee for the benefit of a named person or other "beneficiary."

Under the law, legal title and ownership of the trust corpus passes from the grantor to the trust. Control of these assets is vested in the trustee so long as the trust exists. The trust beneficiary receives only an equitable title to the income or assets of the trust, as described under the terms of the trust declaration. Powers and duties of a trustee can be broad or narrow according to the trust declaration but should carefully reflect the grantor's intentions as to how the trust is to be used. The grantor may also be the trustee or one of the trustees, but such arrangements impose a strict duty against self-dealing lest the validity of the trust itself be called into question.

In order to create a trust, the grantor must sign a written "declaration" or "indenture," which gives specific details of the trust operation and its income distribution both during the grantor's life and afterward. Numerous court and IRS decisions interpreting such trust documents have given every clause special meaning; therefore the writing of the trust indenture requires expert advice, assistance, and coordination with all other legal arrangements the grantor may have made concerning his or her estate.

THE TRUST CORPUS

What assets should go into a trust? If you have gone to the trouble of creating a trust, an argument can be made that *all* your assets should be transferred to the trust. All real and personal property, including jointly held property, should also be transferred. Depending on tax consequences, which should be carefully considered, all certificates of stock, securities, and other evidences of ownership should be reissued in the trust name. Cash bank account titles should be changed from your name to that of the trust. The trust can be made beneficiary of your life insurance and in some cases your pension plans. In some states, law requires a separate real estate trust, but that is only a matter of paperwork. Business interests, including corporation ownership and partnership interests, can also be placed in the trust, but because of management flexibility, consideration should be given to the creation of a separate trust for business interests.

For those who value privacy, the trust affords a shield from "prying eyes" and those who might otherwise contest a will during probate. The creation of the trust can be done in such a way that its existence is a matter of public record, but the names of the grantor and the beneficiaries are kept private, and trust assets need not be disclosed.

ESTATE PLANNING: THE TRADITIONAL ROLE

Perhaps the greatest usage of trusts occurs in estate planning as an effective way of passing title to property while avoiding lengthy and complicated probate court procedures as well as inheritance taxes. Nationally, probate fees (exclusive of taxes) average from 1 to 15 percent of the gross value of the entire estate, a large sum in many cases. Probate in some states like California can require up to two years to complete.

A trust, especially if operative for several years, is also less likely to be challenged legally compared to a will, which may be more easily contested during probate. And the existence of a trust is an obvious defense to the charge of mental incompetence often used to attack the validity of a will, especially one written late in life.

THE TRUST'S ROLE IN ASSET PROTECTION

There are numerous specific types of trusts, and each type is characterized by different variables included in the trust terms. Each has its own degree of potential asset protection and its own advantages, problems, and tax consequences. At various stages of a person's economic life, one or more of these legal devices may be appropriate, and as circumstances change new ones may well be needed.

I will examine each of these trust types from the perspective of effective asset protection.

The Living Trust

A living trust is just what the term indicates: a trust created while the grantor is living (also known to lawyers as an *inter vivos* trust), which provides for the disposition of the trust assets at the grantor's death. The major benefit is that trust assets avoid probate completely, although they are subject to federal and state estate taxes.

A living trust, in contrast to a testamentary trust, which is created after the grantor's death under the terms of his or her will, is created by the grantor to take effect and operate immediately while he or she is still alive. As we shall see, the living trust avoids many of the probate problems of a testamentary trust.

A "revocable" living trust is an entity to which a grantor voluntarily transfers title to his or her assets but with a string attached. Assets can include property of all kinds—real, personal, or both; insurance policies; a home; an auto; a boat; shares of stock; or ownership of a corporation (a "business trust"). Usually there is one trustee, but more can be named to manage the affairs of the transferred property whose title is held in the name of the trust.

When a trust is revocable, the grantor retains the power during his or her lifetime to vary the trust terms, withdraw assets, or even end the trust entirely by formal revocation. To be blunt, such a trust offers little in the way of solid asset protection, especially if the grantor is also the beneficiary during life—a cozy arrangement sure to be challenged by creditors, probably successfully. Upon the death of the grantor, a revocable living trust immediately becomes irrevocable, and the grantor's creditors are out of luck. Under its terms, the trust is thereafter administered by the trustees for the benefit of the named residual beneficiaries.

There are real benefits to a revocable living trust, the most obvious being the grantor's ability to manage the trust assets during his or her lifetime and the option to end the trust whenever changed circumstances may dictate. There is no legal prohibition against the grantor serving as trustee and also being a beneficiary, so long as there are one or more other beneficiaries at the time of the grantor's death. But as a general rule, this incestuous game of same grantor/trustee/beneficiary opens the entire arrangement to creditor assault.

Other than his or her ability to arrange for the desired provision for family or others, the grantor usually receives no real immediate additional financial benefits from such a trust—though there can be many indirect advantages, such as shifting expenses for medical, educational, and other family costs to an entity that is legally insulated against most outside attacks or at least those more difficult and costly for creditors to pursue.

But when a spouse or heirs are beneficiaries, there are many benefits to the living trust in addition to acquiring immediate income from trust assets. These advantages include avoiding judicial probate with the attendant expense and time delays (trust property is not included in the grantor's personal estate); allowing the uninterrupted operation of a family business placed in trust; avoiding public scrutiny of personal financial matters; causing no temporary stop in income for beneficiaries during probate; allowing the grantor an initial choice of the most advantageous law to govern the trust. (The trust can be created in any state jurisdiction, and some states, Delaware for example, are far more flexible than others when it comes to trust law.)

The one great disadvantage with a revocable trust is that it provides very little asset protection. Federal and state trust laws generally restrict the nature and extent of benefits and control that a grantor can retain after creating his or her own trust. This is reflected in a principle of trust law stating that when a grantor retains any degree of control over assets allegedly transferred to a trust, then those assets may remain within ultimate reach of the grantor's creditors. Great reliance has been placed on this legal principle by courts examining the actual manner of trust operation, and this test has upset even the best-intentioned trust plans. The major charge made by creditors against grantors of trusts, which courts are sympathetic to, is that the trust is a smoke screen to avoid payment of the grantors' just debts or judgments.

In 10 states, there are laws that state that a grantor who retains an absolute power of revocation is deemed to be the owner of the trust property, for the purpose of creditors and purchasers. These include Alabama, Indiana, Kansas, Michigan, Minnesota, North Dakota, Ohio, Oklahoma, South Dakota, and Wisconsin. Case law in many other states has opened revocable trust arrangements to similar creditor attachment.

Revocable Living Trusts

A living trust can provide asset protection in spite of the statutes and court decisions just mentioned that place great emphasis on the factor of revocability.

If two revocable living trusts are created, one for each spouse, the husband, who may be engaged in a profession or business in which he is particularly vulnerable to lawsuits (and who isn't these days?), can transfer to his wife's trust title to their home and personal property, which otherwise would be open to his judgment creditors. Repeatedly, courts have upheld the separate nature of a wife's own acquired property from her husband's creditors, unless such transfers are obviously done to defraud creditors. Since 1874, by federal statute the property of either spouse has been relieved from responsibility for the other spouse's separate debts incurred during marriage. And a wife's revocable living trust is her personal property and is thus immune from attack for her husband's obligations. Note that I am talking about more than just putting property "in the wife's name" to protect assets but rather having title passed to the wife's living trust, a far more secure position should a court start scrutinizing assets at the behest of irate creditors.

Irrevocable Living Trusts

A living trust also may be expressly created as "irrevocable" denying a grantor the ultimate control over the assets transferred to the trust once the trust is created.

As a protection against asset attachment, this is virtually perfect because the donor no longer has title to the property or any ability to reacquire it. The only possibility of successful attack by creditors might occur if the transfer can be proven to be fraudulent in some way.

Irrevocability is the trust's unique feature, and a court that finds irrevocability will usually rule that the trust assets are shielded from the grantor's creditors. But irrevocability is also a major disadvantage—if circumstances change, the trust cannot be changed to meet them.

There are also other factors that strengthen the irrevocable living trust as an asset protector. These include having a legitimate reason for the trust creation apart from simple avoidance of creditors' demands, which can be logical estate planning, reasonable provision for spouse and children, and the like.

103

In an irrevocable trust, the exercise of the trustee's powers should be independent, and trust terms should not allow distribution of income to the grantor as a beneficiary. Thus courts have held that although a third person may do so, a grantor cannot set up his own spendthrift trust immune from creditors. Any distribution of trust assets at the grantor's death should go to a designated class of beneficiaries, for example, spouse and children. The grantor should not serve as the trustee; a person who is completely independent should. In other words, the trust must be real in every sense, not just a fake arrangement allowing the grantor a life-long free ride from judgment creditors.

It is worth noting that many courts and now more than a few legislatures have begun to measure the vulnerability of trust assets in strict terms of a trust's revocability. Since 1987, for example, California statutes have allowed creditors to reach trust assets when the grantor has retained the power to revoke the trust and to reach trust payments to the grantor, who is also a beneficiary.

Tax Advantages of a Living Trust

Under the law, the income and assets of a revocable or irrevocable trust are subject to state and federal death taxes. But these trusts can be arranged so that upon the subsequent deaths of named beneficiaries or their heirs, further death taxes can be avoided, which is a real savings for the trust beneficiaries, though this helpful aspect is often distant in time.

For example, the living trust can realize significant tax savings, especially if two trusts are created, one by each spouse, for the benefit of their children. Using the $600,000 federal estate tax exemption available to each parent, $1.2 million in death taxes can be avoided as compared to a tax of $235,000 on an estate received as a straight inheritance. These trusts can be structured to give the surviving spouse the benefit of the other

104

spouse's trust until that survivor dies, then both trusts can continue for the children, or the assets can be distributed to them.

Again, I emphasize the great importance of creating and operating a living trust within the strict letter of the law. Title to property must be deeded to the trust, and the trustee must manage assets for the benefit of the named beneficiaries. All transactions must be formally correct and records carefully maintained. As I have repeatedly said, there is a substantial body of case law in which the IRS has challenged successfully defective or sham trusts as no more than evasive devices to avoid tax liability—and these are the factors that courts scrutinize.

The Testamentary Trust

The most common form of trust is a testamentary trust, the terms of which the grantor includes in his or her last will to take effect after death. This method allows provision for loved ones, especially when the grantor has concerns about a minor beneficiary's ability to manage his or her own affairs. Such concerns have given rise to the testamentary creation of the so-called spendthrift trust, the assets of which are immune from attacks by the beneficiary's creditors.

Although they are popular, testamentary trusts have distinct disadvantages often unexplained by legal advisors. Estate and income taxes must be paid at the death of the grantor, although successive estate tax levies can often be avoided as trust property passes to beneficiaries and their heirs in later years. Testamentary trusts do not avoid initial probate and sometimes are subjected to continuous court supervision, which often entails great legal expense. Because they are subject to probate, the activity of the testamentary trust and its trustee is a matter of public record and scrutiny for all to see.

In addition to trusts being created by wills, trusts can be created formally by contract between two or more parties

105

(express trusts), or when title to real or personal property is involved by a deed of trust. An implied trust may result in the absence of a formal trust when a court finds its creation from factual circumstances, as when one spouse consistently places property in the name of the other.

The Business Trust

A type of trust once popular in America is the so-called business trust or Massachusetts trust, named after the state in which it first appeared in 1856. It has also been called a "common law trust" because it does not depend on statutory authorization for its creation. This hybrid legal device is unique because it is designed to operate a business, produce a profit, and protect business and personal assets as compared to conventional trusts, which are used simply for asset protection and passive income production.

Partaking of some characteristics of both a partnership and a corporation, the business trust is a voluntary association of trustees who actively hold title to property and operate a business under the terms of a joint trust agreement for the benefit of shareholders who own the trust and share in the profits. If the shareholders actually exercise control over the business together with the trustees, they too become personally responsible for the liabilities of the trust. If shareholders exercise no control, they are personally exempt from creditor attack.

This arrangement is somewhat like a corporation but is easier to form since it requires no formal registration with the state, only a signed agreement among the parties. Since this trust is entirely private, it can avoid many government reporting requirements and conceal the actual owners. The business trust was often used as a means to escape foreign business registration in other states and laws restricting the sale of securities. At one time the business trust was not taxed as a separate entity, thus avoiding the double taxation imposed on corporate income, but tax law changes imposing income taxes on trusts have largely removed this advantage.

The greatest disadvantage of the business trust is that shareholders, if they are active in the business, can be held personally liable for trust debts to the extent of their investment. Conversely, shareholder trust interests can be attached by their personal creditors.

But there are asset protection possibilities in the business trust. Consider a situation in which a business is run by a father, who is obviously exposed to personal liability for potential business claims or other litigation. His family's home, bank accounts, and other assets could be deeded to a business trust to which he has no ownership but is the managing trustee. This gives him 100 percent control of his business and exempts the trust assets of the beneficial owners, his nonparticipatory wife and children, from creditor attack.

While the business trust arrangement has some limited potential value as an asset protection device, there are many other methods discussed here that are better suited to that role without mixing asset protection with the unpredictability of an active business enterprise.

The International Asset Protection Trust

In the last decade, a novel asset protection device also in trust form has gained some popularity. It is known as an international asset protection trust (APT). This foreign-based trust, if properly arranged, can be very advantageous to persons who can afford the costs of its creation and annual maintenance—wealthy people who want to shield their personal assets from demanding creditors, protracted litigation, and other potentially unpleasant liabilities, even an ex-spouse bent on revenge.

A Word to the Wise

If you are seriously considering creating a personal foreign asset protection trust, there is one important fact that must be fully understood and accepted: this arrangement will only succeed if planned and created prospectively at a time of financial calm. Not only will it not work if attempted in response to a pending personal fiscal crisis, but taking such a step may make things far worse.

If the foreign trust is hastily established when you are about to be (or have been) sued or forced into personal bankruptcy, the act of transferring your assets to a foreign entity is likely to violate strict civil and criminal fraudulent conveyance laws designed to protect creditors. These laws allow a court to declare a trust or any device used to conceal or remove assets from creditors as illegal—null and void. If your assets remain within an American court's jurisdiction, your conveyance of title to a foreign trustee is unlikely to protect them from domestic attachment. If the assets are physically within the foreign jurisdiction, as in the case of funds in an offshore bank account, the creditor will definitely have more difficulty reaching them before you can act to protect the funds, but the establishment of such an account after litigation begins is also strong evidence of fraud.

In litigation-mad America, the sensible business or professional person does not wait for the day of disaster to begin planning asset protection. Medical, legal, and professional malpractice suits as well as legislative and judicial imposition of no-fault personal liability on corporate officers and directors have by now become a fact of business life. An active business or professional person can suddenly be held personally responsible for all sorts of unforeseen events, such as a company's environmental pollution, a bank failure, or simply a dissatisfied client. If proof were needed of the seriousness of the situation, note that premiums for all types of malpractice insurance have gone through the roof. In this business climate, astute people must consider the best way to protect their personal assets against any eventuality.

The Up Front Cost

There is another important factor to consider before deciding to create an offshore trust. Because a foreign jurisdiction is the situs of such a trust, the cost of creating an average asset protection trust abroad usually exceeds $15,000 initially, plus several thousand dollars in annual maintenance fees. Unless the total assets you seek to shield are worth more than $2 million, such a trust may not be practical because of its creation costs.

Typical advice from lawyers and trust companies is that you should have a net worth of $500,000 or more to justify the expense of a foreign asset protection trust, since some expert's fees for establishing and administering such trusts have run as high as $50,000 and trust administration fees usually involve a percentage of the total value of the assets being handled by the trustee.

A Strong Creditor Deterrent

Given the need for protection and understanding timing and the potential cost, you can indeed deal with the threat to your hard-earned assets by placing them beyond the reach of potential domestic litigation plaintiffs, creditors, and contingent-fee lawyers in an asset protection trust located in a foreign country where the law favors your goals.

Certain foreign jurisdictions do not grant legal recognition to U.S. or other nondomestic court orders. In such a case, an American creditor bent on collection will be forced to relitigate completely (in the foreign national court and after hiring foreign lawyers) the original claim that gave rise to the American judgment. The sheer complexity and cost of such a foreign collection effort is likely to stop all but the most determined adversaries.

Where To Establish Your APT

If you are considering creating a foreign asset protection trust, you should find out whether the prospective foreign jurisdiction's laws are favorable, clear, and truly offer the shelter you seek. Examine the recent record of economic and political stability of the country, the reputation of its judicial system, local tax laws, the general business climate, possible language barriers, and the state of available communication and financial facilities. Unfortunately, there are very few qualified American experts in the field of asset protection law, and you should proceed with caution before choosing your financial advisor for this important project.

Several offshore financial centers are located in nations that purposely have developed and tailored their laws to be hospitable to foreign-owned asset protection trusts. Among these are the Caribbean area nations of the Cayman Islands known as the Bahamas, Belize, and the Turks and Caicos Islands; in the South Pacific, the Cook Islands, a protectorate of nearby New Zealand; the Isle of Man, a British protectorate off the coast of Scotland; and Cyprus and Gibraltar at either end of the Mediterranean.

The greatest worry about a foreign asset protection trust is often the distance between you and your assets and the people who manage them. As I said, although assets need not be transferred physically to the foreign country in which the trust exists, circumstances may dictate such a precautionary transfer. There is always a justified concern about choosing people whom you feel you can rely on to create and assist you in managing the trust. This is definitely a situation in which requesting references is in order, and they should be checked carefully.

The country in which you choose to locate your trust must have local legal experts who understand fully and have the ability to assist you properly in accomplishing your objectives. The foreign local attorney who creates your trust unquestionably must know the applicable local and American law and tax consequences, or you will be in trouble from the start. All of the countries named have developed such legal and banking professionals.

Operating Your Foreign APT

Once established, the offshore asset protection trust in its basic form can consist of little more than a trust account in an international bank located in a foreign country. Many well-established multinational banks provide trustees for such arrangements and have staff experienced in such matters. With today's instant communications and international banking facilities, it is as convenient to hold assets and accounts overseas as it is in an American city. Most international banks have dollar-denominated accounts, often with better interest rates than United States financial institutions offer.

Generally, it is advisable to transfer only cash and intangible assets, such as stocks, bonds, and securities, to a foreign trust. Portable assets, such as gold coins or diamonds, can also be transferred. Transferring the title to real estate or a business located in the United States to a foreign trust is questionable. Transferring a paper title does nothing to keep these assets away from American creditors because of the physical location of the real property. An attempted transfer could make the foreign trust subject to the jurisdiction of an American court, which could use the transfer as justification to find that the trust is doing business in the United States.

Depending on the country of choice, you, as a grantor of the foreign asset protection trust, can gain many advantages, including the exercise of far greater control over assets and income from the trust than permitted under domestic American trust law. Generally, the American rule forbidding the creation of a trust by a grantor for his own benefit does not apply in foreign countries.

Creation of such a trust, as I said, will discourage domestic American creditors faced with the tangle of enforcing a U.S. judgment in a foreign country where asset protection trusts are legally recognized and protected. Foreign law usually does not support the strict application of American fraudulent conveyance law, and in some countries a creditor's suit must be brought within two years of the date on which the foreign trust was established or the case will not even be considered.

Using an APT for International Investment

A foreign trust can also be used for international investment activity. Your foreign trustee handles the investments and paperwork while you make long-distance investment suggestions. In this way, you can take advantage of the world's best investment opportunities without worrying about borders or conflicting laws. A foreign trust with a lawyer or trust company as trustee in the offshore country is an excellent way to achieve international diversification of your investments.

Additionally, the trust can provide privacy, confidentiality, and reduced domestic reporting requirements in the United States; avoidance of domestic taxes and probate in case of death; and increased flexibility in conducting affairs in cases of disability, transferring assets, international investing, or avoiding domestic currency controls. Of course, a foreign asset protection trust can also substitute for or supplement costly professional liability insurance or even a prenuptial agreement, offering strong protection of your assets for your heirs and their inheritance.

Offshore Trust Creation

The structure of a foreign asset protection trust differs little from that of an American trust. The grantor or settlor creates the trust by transferring title to his assets to the trust to be administered by the trustees, according to the trust declaration, for the named beneficiaries. Usually, foreign law requires the naming of three trustees (the grantor usually may not be one)—two located in the United States and one independent managing trustee in the foreign country. The trust declaration can allow the grantor to replace the foreign trustee at any time with another nominee and may also require the grantor's prior approval of investments or distributions. Beneficiaries can vary according to the settlor's estate planning objectives, and the grantor may be a beneficiary but usually not the primary one. Foreign trust law, unlike strict American "arm's length" requirements, allows a nonnational grantor to receive income and benefits from the trust while maintaining effective control over the investment and distribution of the trust principal.

Many foreign jurisdictions also permit appointment of a local "trust protector" who, as the title indicates, oversees the operation of the trust to ensure that its objectives are met and the law is followed. A protector does not manage the trust but can veto actions in some cases.

In most of these countries, nothing is required to be registered with the government. The trust agreement and the parties involved are not required to be disclosed, and the information filed is not available as part of a public record. In these privacy-conscious countries, the trustee is allowed to reveal information about the trust only in very limited circumstances and then usually only by local court order.

United States Tax Consequences

Under American tax laws, although foreign asset protection trusts themselves are tax-neutral, they are usually considered the same as domestic trusts, meaning income from the trust is treated as the grantor's personal income and taxed to him or her as reportable annual income.

Because the grantor retains some degree of control over the transfer of his assets to the foreign trust, American gift taxes on the transfer of assets to the trust can usually be avoided. At death, estate taxes are

113

imposed on the value of trust assets for the grantor's estate, but all existing exemptions, such as those for martial assets, can be used. Asset protection trusts are usually not subject to the 35 percent U.S. excise tax imposed on transfers of property to a "foreign person," a point to be explored more fully below.

Under American law, you, as grantor or beneficiary, must disclose the existence of a trust on your federal tax return, but creditors must obtain a court order to gain access to your tax returns, and that takes time.

Avoiding Income Tax on APT Income

Under section 679 of the U.S. Internal Revenue Code, when four conditions are met, the grantor of a foreign trust can be taxed annually on all income and gains earned by the trust, even if they are undistributed. In other words, when you put money or property in the trust, all income earned by the trust is included in your gross income as though the trust did not exist.

If you plan to use the trust only for asset protection, privacy, or international diversification, this probably will not matter to you. However, if you plan to use the trust for investment purposes (and why should you not?), you should know the four factors that cause a grantor to be treated as owner of an offshore trust and taxed on its income. This occurs when:

1) a United States person transfers assets, including cash, to a foreign trust;
2) the transfer to the trust is made either directly or indirectly from the United States person;
3) the trust has one or more United States beneficiaries; and
4) the trust is organized and located in a foreign country.

114

Elimination of any *one* of these factors allows an American grantor to escape U.S. income taxes on the trust income.

The easiest thing to change in order to avoid the tax is to not have the offshore trust established by a "United States person," a phrase which is broadly defined in the tax code to mean a U.S. citizen, resident alien, partnership, corporation, estate or trust. To take advantage of this loophole, the grantor of the foreign trust must be a foreigner.

This can be accomplished by having a foreign corporation set up the foreign trust. In order to maximize the American tax benefits, the true grantor can form a foreign corporation and transfer assets to that corporation. Then the corporation as grantor forms a foreign trust and transfers its assets to the trust. The beneficiary of the trust can be a U.S. citizen or resident, usually the true grantor's spouse, child, or grandchild. The corporate grantor retains the power to change the beneficiary, revoke the trust, and control disposition of the trust property. The American beneficiaries are not taxed when they receive income from the trust because the corporate grantor is the owner and as such is responsible for taxes. Since the trust and all its assets are located outside the United States, the corporate grantor, which is also foreign, need not file a U.S. tax return. If the trust is located in a tax haven, there may be no tax imposed at all.

There is another way to avoid being taxed on the income earned by the offshore trust. Note the third factor in the list above. The offshore trust rules apply only when the trust has a United States beneficiary. If there is none, the grantor is not taxed on the trust income. Simply set up the trust to benefit someone who is not an American citizen or resident, or have an offshore corporation as the beneficiary of the offshore trust. Under the Internal Revenue Code, an offshore corporation is not considered a United States beneficiary of a foreign trust unless 50 percent or more of the corporation's voting

115

power is controlled by United States persons. So if a United States person is one of several persons you want to benefit from the trust, you can have the beneficiaries form an offshore corporation. Be sure the United States person or persons do not own more than 50 percent of the voting stock. If these conditions are met, a true grantor will fall outside the offshore trust income tax rules and no tax will be imposed on the trust income. Income can remain in the foreign trust and continue to accumulate tax-free.

There is yet another method by which U.S. taxes on income from a foreign trust can be avoided, but you, as grantor, will not be around to enjoy it. The offshore trust income tax rules are avoided when the foreign trust is created as a testamentary trust under the terms of a last will. Neither your estate nor any other United States person who is named as beneficiary of the trust can then be taxed as grantor of the trust.

This loophole allows income to accumulate tax-free in the foreign trust. The trust can invest anywhere in the world, including the United States, and pay little or no taxes depending on where the investments are made and how they are structured. If your children do not need the income or assets of your estate immediately, the foreign testamentary trust can make their eventual inheritance much larger than it otherwise would be.

Avoid the Excise Tax on Foreign Transfers

In transferring assets to a foreign asset protection trust, there is one more tax hurdle to clear—the excise tax imposed on some transfers of property to foreign entities. This tax is imposed by section 1491 of the Internal Revenue Code (with exceptions stated in section 1492) on transfers by a United States person or entity to a foreign corporation, partnership, estate, or trust.

A 35 percent tax is imposed on any appreciation in value of the property from its original basis and not otherwise recognized in the transfer. In other words, if you transfer appreciated property to a foreign trust, the transfer becomes taxable, and you must pay either the regular capital gains tax or the 35 percent excise tax.

Obviously, the easy way to avoid the excise tax is to transfer cash or nonappreciated property to the foreign entity.

Foreign or Offshore Corporations

Since I mentioned the possibility of avoiding U.S. taxes by using a foreign asset protection trust in conjunction with a foreign corporation, let's take a closer look at the latter entity so there will be no illusions about its overall usefulness.

There have always been investment experts who claim the perfect repository for assets in need of protection is a corporation chartered in a foreign nation (an offshore corporation), which you, as the instigator, control through various indirect means.

Theoretically, your foreign corporate ownership will be concealed from the United States and other governments, allowing you financial privacy while the corporation invests in foreign mutual funds or other valuable assets located outside the United States, thus sheltering income and profits from American taxes. Company business can be conducted through a designated nominee, further shielding your secret participation from creditors or the IRS.

In theory this sounds grand, but there are many practical problems associated with an offshore corporation, not the least of which is compliance with U.S. law.

First, as in establishing any domestic corporation, legal formalities must be strictly followed when incorporating abroad, and the costs of setting up and maintaining a foreign company can be considerable. You need experienced local in-country legal counsel that understands your asset protection objectives. Corporations anywhere are rule-bound creatures requiring separate books and records, meetings, min-

117

utes, and authorizing resolutions, all making it less flexible than other arrangements.

Then there are the problems presented by U.S. court decisions interpreting the obligations of an American actively involved in a foreign corporation.

There are separate U.S. taxes on unrealized gains and on income from and capital gains accrued on property transferred to a foreign corporation. If the offshore company can be characterized as a "foreign personal holding company" as defined by the IRS, an American shareholder's portion of undistributed earnings will be taxed to him as ordinary income each year. The same IRS rules apply if the offshore entity qualifies as a "controlled foreign corporation," but in this case additional taxes are imposed on any gain derived from the sale of the corporate assets.

For those who seek the quiet secrecy a foreign corporation allegedly offers, there is an impressive series of cases in which U.S. courts have pierced the offshore corporate veil, attributing "constructive ownership" to the involved U.S. taxpayer as an individual. Similar judicial findings of actual control have been based on a "chain of entities" linking the U.S. taxpayer to the offshore corporation. American courts consistently identify the person who has substantive control as compared to paper nominees exercising nominal control.

To add to these complications, there are various specific IRS reporting requirements imposed on a U.S. taxpayer who serves as an officer, director, or 10 percent or greater shareholder in a foreign personal holding company or offshore corporation of any kind. The U.S. Supreme Court has ruled that a U.S. taxpayer can be held guilty of "falsifying a federal income tax return" by falsely maintaining he has no foreign corporate holdings. Further, the Court said that Fourth Amendment guarantees regarding searches and seizures do not apply to documents located abroad pertaining to a U.S. taxpayer's ownership of foreign interests. When American courts conclude offshore

118

corporations are being used to conceal assets or avoid taxes, they levy additional dollar penalties plus interest and can impose criminal convictions as well.

This is not to say foreign corporations have no place in asset protection planning, but U.S. taxpayers should have no illusions about the legal and tax limitations that apply to them if they are involved as incorporators, officers, directors, shareholders, or simply as beneficiaries of corporate acts.

Foreign Trust Tax Summary

Foreign asset protection trusts can also be extremely flexible financial and tax planning devices. Though federal government efforts have been made to eliminate these trust tax benefits, opportunities still remain. Remember that offshore trust strategies are complicated and full of pitfalls, so when you venture abroad financially, go armed with the expert assistance of an experienced international tax and legal adviser whose only loyalty is to you.

11 The Swiss Annuity: Judgment-Proof and a High Return

One of the most important financial sectors of the Swiss economy is the insurance industry. Like Swiss banks, insurance companies are conservative and provide excellent safety for investors. In the past 130 years not a single insurance company has failed—this is a record that even Swiss banks envy.

The insurance industry in Switzerland benefits from both unique tax advantages and knowledgeable and conservative management. This combination leads to solid and surprisingly productive investment opportunities. Some people equate a conservative approach to investments with low or marginal returns, but this is not the case with Swiss insurance companies. The returns from these companies are quite high because the companies seldom have to deduct losses on bad investments, which decreases the yield. Without losses, it is possible to maintain a conservative approach to investment with high returns.

Switzerland has only about 20 insurance companies. All of them are very solid and well managed. Swiss insurance companies do not engage in rate competition but instead focus their energies on maintaining their strength. Because the insurance industry is somewhat concentrated, it is on the whole stronger and easier to supervise than the insurance industry in the United States, where there are thousands of companies to regulate.

The Swiss Federal Bureau of Private Insurance regulates the insurance industry in Switzerland and has the reputation of being strict. A clause in the Swiss federal constitution in 1885 established this regulation. Because the Swiss government regulates the insurance industry tightly, as it does with all of the finance industry, investments in any of the products offered by Swiss insurance companies carry an extremely low risk. Indeed, they have been described by some as having no risk at all. For example, liquidity and valuation of investments are ultraconservative. A maximum of 30 percent of investible funds may be put in real estate. This is a very low percentage, especially in a country where real estate has always held high value. Consequently, exposure to any downturn in real estate prices is limited.

During the '80s and into the early '90s, undoubtedly many American banks and insurance companies were sorry they did not follow a real estate investment policy like their Swiss counterparts. And if the banks and insurance companies aren't wishing it, certainly their policyholders are because when the value of real estate dropped virtually throughout America, the value of many investments dropped accordingly. Some portfolios that were overextended in real estate were ruined.

The Swiss insurance companies go a step further in an effort to protect their investors. They often carry their real estate holdings at less than half of their present market value. This wide margin allows for a significant downward spiral in prices and value in real estate before the safety of investments is affected.

The Swiss also handle their accounting in a conservative manner. Unlike many American companies that tend to overvalue assets in order to achieve high prices

122

in the stock market, Swiss insurance companies frequently have hidden reserves of millions of dollars.

Swiss insurance companies offer a variety of investment opportunities. Many offer more products than Swiss banks do. Perhaps one of the best products offered by Swiss insurance companies is the annuity.

Although most investors have heard of annuities, many do not realize the excellent opportunities for growth that annuities, particularly Swiss annuities, offer. An annuity is an investment vehicle that enables the investor to set money aside for retirement or other objectives in a tax-advantaged plan. One of the most important benefits of annuities is that they permit the investor to defer taxes on his or her savings, thereby building assets faster than can be done in other investments. Although annuities can be used to put money aside for various purposes, most often they are associated with retirement accounts.

This is not a coincidence. Several features make annuities especially attractive for a retirement plan:

- In a true annuity there is no investment ceiling. Although IRAs (Individual Retirement Accounts) are special tax-advantaged plans where taxes are deferred until assets are drawn out, the amount that can be contributed each year is limited.
- Annuities provide the advantage of tax-deferral. Money grows faster in an annuity than in other investments with similar rates of return because interest as well as money that would be used to pay taxes accumulates in the account. An added feature is the likelihood that the investor, if he or she waits to take the money out after retirement, will be in a lower tax bracket. This will also save money.
- Annuities provide excellent security for the

123

investor's family. If the annuity owner dies before the earnings of the annuity are distributed, his or her beneficiaries can receive the full value of the annuity. In some instances, by naming a beneficiary the annuity may be able to bypass probate and avoid the resultant costs.

- Investing in annuities is easy. Record-keeping is little more than monitoring the statements you periodically receive. There are no annual IRS forms to file, and you need provide no entry on Form 1040 until the payments begin, which in most cases is at retirement.

Annuities may not be the most exciting investments, but they are one of the financial industry's fastest growing products. Although annuities have been available since the early 1970s, the last few years have witnessed an explosion in the growth of annuity sales.

In the United States, for instance, sales of domestic annuities are approximately $50 billion per year. As the American population ages, it is realizing that annuities are necessary to plan for retirement and are one of the best investment alternatives available. Many people perceive annuities as an investment that can help them to remain self-sufficient throughout their retirement years.

Sometimes people confuse annuities with mutual funds. There is an important difference. An annuity can offer investment growth similar to a mutual fund, but it defers taxes until retirement. A mutual fund does not. The annuity plans, of which there are many, can be structured so that once the investor begins to draw on the funds, the annuity makes regular payments for life.

Although the investor doesn't own the investments the annuity makes, he benefits from their investment. Since the insurance company owns the investment, the investor's savings can grow with all the gains being tax-deferred. This is an advantage that owners of most mutual funds are prevented from taking. When an investor buys a mutual fund, at the end of the year he or she pays a capital gains distribution. Even if the investor reinvests the gains, this is a taxable event. With an annuity, however, any profit made that is left in the annuity continues to grow in a tax-deferred state.

Since annuities are products of insurance companies, the fees paid by the investor are different than the fees paid for mutual funds. For most annuities, there are no front-end load fees or commissions. Instead, there are "surrender" charges for investors who withdraw funds early in an American annuity. Surrender charges apply usually during the first five or six years. It should be noted that this is not the case in Swiss annuities, which will be discussed later.

Annuities offer the best benefits of other similar investment alternatives. For example, they contain some of the tax-deferred benefits of IRAs and employer-sponsored 401(k) plans. Just as with an IRA, as long as gains made from the investment remain in the annuity account, no taxes are due. Not only does this help savings to grow faster, but it allows the individual investor some control over when he or she will pay taxes. Taxes are due when money is withdrawn. Similar to an IRA or 401(k) account, if you withdraw funds from an annuity before the age of 59, you will be subject to a 10 percent penalty.

However, annuities offer much more than either the IRA or 401(k)—there is no limit to how much you can invest. Furthermore, since an annuity is a product of an insurance company, you will receive a guaranteed regular income after retirement no matter how long you might live.

In an IRA or similar retirement account, initial investments are made before taxes under certain conditions. This permits the investor to shield some of his or her current income from taxes. It also allows investments to grow tax-deferred. Although with an annuity the initial investment is made with dollars after taxes, the annuity

125

has no investment limit and investment gains are tax-free until withdrawn. While IRAs and 401(k) plans are sound investment options and should not be overlooked for retirement planning, the wise investor is well aware that the amount that can be contributed to such plans is limited. Over the long run this holds down growth.

When annuities are compared to other investment alternatives, especially when one is looking for an investment to accumulate savings for retirement, annuities clearly are the product of choice. Because the interest grows tax-free until funds are withdrawn, the returns are higher than similar taxable investment options. Also, when the owner of the annuity takes money out typically at retirement, he or she is in a lower tax bracket and thus pays less taxes on money that has been growing tax-deferred. Annuities without question are safe, solid investments.

SOME ADVANTAGES OF SWISS ANNUITIES

Not all annuities are the same. Unlike those in the United States, Swiss annuities are heavily regulated in an effort to avoid any potential problems. Frankly, Swiss annuities reduce the risks that United States annuities carry. Swiss annuities are denominated in the solid Swiss franc (SFr), which is backed by gold, while United States annuities are backed by the dollar, which has been losing purchasing power throughout this entire century. Additionally, the Swiss payout is guaranteed.

Swiss annuities are attractive for other reasons as well. They are exempt from the 35 percent withholding tax that Switzerland imposes on bank account interest received by foreigners. Moreover, Swiss annuities do not have to be reported to Swiss or U.S. tax authorities.

American buyers of Swiss annuities are required to pay a 1 percent U.S. federal excise tax on the purchase of the policy. You might liken this to the tax rule that requires Americans who shop in a state with a lower sales tax than their own to pay the difference in sales tax to their own state. (This is particularly true in regard to mail order sales.)

The U.S. federal excise tax form (IRS Form 720) requires only a calculation of 1 percent tax of any foreign policies purchased. It does not require details of the policy or from whom it was bought. The tax is paid only once at the time of purchase, and it is the responsibility of the U.S. citizen to report the policy. It is important to note that Swiss insurance companies do not report purchasing information—not the purchase of the policy, the payments into the policy, or the interest or dividends earned—to any government agency in Switzerland or the United States.

Payments of Swiss annuities are flexible and can be arranged to fit the investor's needs. Although annuity payments are denominated in Swiss francs, the investor may receive them in any currency he or she wishes. Payments can be converted at the investor's bank in Switzerland, or the investor may instruct the insurance company to make the conversion. Payments can be received annually, every six months, or quarterly. Although a monthly option is available, it is restricted to Swiss residents. Payments can be sent anywhere in the world or to a bank of the investor's choice. Most North Americans prefer to receive their annuity payments by check in dollars.

One of the mainstays of Swiss annuity plans is their confidentiality. Another is their safety. A third is their flexibility. Together these factors combine to make Swiss annuities excellent investment choices. But there are even more reasons to choose Swiss annuities.

MORE BENEFITS OF SWISS ANNUITIES

Swiss annuities offer a variety of important benefits to investors. Following are some of the most valuable.

Competitive Interest Rates and Dividends
You will find that Swiss annuities pay excellent rates and dividends compared to similar investments.

Famous Swiss Financial Safety
Switzerland is financially one of the soundest (if not *the* soundest) countries in the world. Its currency is backed by gold and is considered to be the most solid among the world's industrialized nations. The Swiss insurance industry has not had a failure in the 130 years it has been in operation.

No Foreign Reporting Requirements
As with all their financial transactions, the Swiss elevate privacy to a high priority. A Swiss annuity is not a "foreign bank account" and therefore is not subject to the reporting requirements on the IRS Form 1040 or on the special U.S. Treasury form for reporting foreign bank accounts. Furthermore, at this time, transfers of funds to Switzerland by check or wire are not reported to any government agency either by the sender or the bank. The reporting requirements apply only to cash and cash equivalents, including items such as money orders, cashier's checks, and traveler's checks.

No Forced Repatriation of Funds
Some investors pay little attention to exchange rates and controls, but those very rates and controls can exercise a major impact on the profitability of one's investments. Suppose that the U.S. government was to institute exchange controls that required overseas investments to be repatriated to the United States. This has happened often in the past with other nations whenever governments have imposed exchange controls. Insurance policies would likely not be covered under any forced repatriation because they are considered to be a pending contract between the investor and the

128

insurance company. (Note that Swiss bank accounts would probably not escape such controls.)

Instant Liquidity

With the SwissPlus annuity plan, which is described later, an investor can liquidate up to 100 percent of his or her account without penalty after the first year. During the first year, there is a SFr500 charge.

Protection from Creditors

Swiss annuities are entirely protected from a host of creditors. If the annuity purchaser's wife or children are named as beneficiaries, no creditor, including the IRS, may seize or attach the annuity and no liens may be attached to the annuity in any way. Thus, the investor is assured that the wealth contained in his or her annuity cannot be touched by any individual or government agency, and the funds in his or her annuity will in fact go to designated heirs.

No Swiss Tax

Swiss franc annuities are free from Swiss taxes. If, however, the investor accumulates Swiss francs through other types of investments, he or she will be subject to the 35 percent withholding tax on interest or dividends earned in Switzerland. The investor enjoys similar tax advantages in the United States, where insurance proceeds are not taxed, and earnings on annuities during the tax-deferred period are not taxable until the income is paid or the annuity is liquidated.

No Load Fees

Investment in Swiss annuities offers the advantage of no load fees, front-end or back-end. In addition, the investor can cancel at any time without a loss of principal and with all principal, interest, and dividends

129

payable if canceled after one year. If the investor cancels during the first year, he or she is subject to a small penalty of about 500 Swiss francs plus the loss of interest.

Qualified or United States Pension Plans

Swiss annuities can be placed in various United States tax-sheltered plans, including IRAs, Keogh, or corporate plans. Such plans can also be rolled over into a Swiss annuity. If you wish to put a Swiss annuity in a United States pension plan, the only thing required is a United States trustee—a bank or similar institution—and that the annuity contract be held in the United States by that trustee. For a minimal administration fee many banks offer "self-directed" pension plans, which can easily be used for this purpose.

Convenience

Managing a Swiss annuity is as easy as managing an annuity in the United States. You can send your deposits to Switzerland in the form of a personal check in dollars. To send the envelope overseas, you need 50 cents postage (at the time of this writing), or you may transfer funds by bank wire.

SWISSPLUS: THE SWISS ANNUITY OF CHOICE

First offered in 1991, SwissPlus is a new annuity product that combines the benefits of Swiss bank accounts and Swiss deferred annuities. Having eliminated even the most minor drawbacks, SwissPlus offers the best of Swiss investment advantages for American investors interested in annuities.

SwissPlus is a convertible annuity account. It is offered only by Elvia Life of Geneva. While other Swiss insurance companies could create and offer annuity products for the international market, they have not done so.

Elvia Life is a rock-solid company. Founded in 1924,

it has $2 billion in assets and serves 220,000 clients, 57 percent of whom live in Switzerland.

Elvia Life offers its clients the option of choosing which currency they wish for their accounts. Annuity accounts may be denominated in the Swiss franc, the dollar, the German mark, or the ECU. (For investors not familiar with the ECU, this refers to the European Currency Unit, a new currency created in 1979 composed of 11 European currencies. Its value fluctuates and is calculated each day by the European Commission in accordance with changes in the values of the underlying currencies. The actual value of the ECU is arrived at through the composition of a weighted mean of all member currencies of the European Monetary System. Because the balance of the ECU changes based on the changes in exchange rates and interest rates between the currencies that make it up, the ECU tends to limit the risks of exchange and interest rates.)

The investor may switch from one currency to the other at any time and without penalty. The investor also has the option of diversifying the account by investing in more than one currency. The investor can change the currency at any time during the accumulation period until he or she begins to receive income or withdraws the capital.

SwissPlus is a unique investment product. Officially labeled an annuity, it functions more like a savings account than a deferred annuity. Since it is sold by an insurance company, it satisfies the IRS's definition of an annuity and accumulates gains tax-free until the plan is converted into an income annuity or is liquidated.

The earnings of SwissPlus are impressive compared to similar products. SwissPlus accounts achieve about the same return as long-term government bonds in the same currency in which the account is denominated (in the case of the ECU, European Union bonds) less a 1/2-percent management fee. Like other Swiss investment

131

products, SwissPlus benefits from the same government regulations. For example, regulations protect investors from both under-performance and overcharging. The Swiss insurance company guarantees both interest and dividend income.

When the account matures, the investor has several options:

1) He or she can select a lump sum payout. In this case, the investor pays a capital gains tax on accumulated earnings only.
2) He or she may roll the funds into an income annuity, in this case paying capital gains taxes only as future income payments are received but only on the portion representing accumulated earnings.
3) The investor may simply extend the scheduled term by giving notice in advance of the originally scheduled date. Choosing this option would allow him or her to continue to defer taxes on accumulated earnings.

Another important feature of SwissPlus is instant liquidity. Most annuities don't offer this. In a SwissPlus account, all capital plus all accumulated interest and dividends are accessible after the first year without penalty. During the first year, 100 percent of the principal is freely accessible less a SFr500 fee and loss of interest. Unlike most American annuities, if you need your funds for an emergency or wish to make another investment, you are not prevented from obtaining your money and you are not subjected to high penalties.

SWISS ANNUITIES AND FLEXIBILITY

Most people buy annuities so they will have a constant source of income during retirement. The Swiss realize that the needs of people differ, so they have developed a variety of options for both single and joint annuities.

When you consider the various options annuities offer, there are several factors you should examine. First, you should consider your age and the age of your spouse when the income from your annuity is likely to begin. You must also consider the amount of the investment you are willing to make. Such factors play a crucial role in the type of annuity you select.

Of all the factors you should examine, age probably has the greatest impact. The older an investor is, the more income difference there is between an annuity without refund and one with any of the beneficiary options. For example, should you purchase an annuity when you are 55, the difference in life income created under each option is not that much because the life expectancy for both men and women at 55 exceeds 25 years. Based on life expectancy and payment rates, the insurance company will likely have to pay out the entire amount of the plan no matter what option the contract contains. Options will have different effects, based on age.

There are many options from which you may choose. Assessing your financial goals and situation is important. Asking yourself questions similar to the ones that follow can prove helpful.

- Who is dependent upon my financial support?
- What is the purpose of my buying an annuity?
- How much money can I open the account with?
- How much money can I invest monthly? Yearly?
- When (based on current considerations and factors) do I plan to take funds out?
- How (based on current considerations and factors) do I plan to take funds out?

Asking yourself such questions can lead you to your best options with an annuity. For example, if you wish to use the annuity to provide income for your spouse someday, then you should consider a plan that does in fact provide for that person. You might consider a joint annuity, a plan called "10 years certain, with refund," or you might decide to take out single annuities, one for you and one for your spouse.

On the other hand, if you have no dependents and are over 65, you may decide on a straight-life annuity that pays you the highest income for as long as you live. In this case there is no need to leave any funds behind. After your death the insurance company stops all payments. You receive the highest income possible for the rest of your life, but there is nothing for beneficiaries.

If you wish to provide for beneficiaries, you should consider annuities "with refund" or "10, 15, or any number of years certain." Each plan has special features.

"With refund" is a plan that at the death of the policyholder, the unused portion of the premium paid is refunded to the beneficiary in a lump sum. The amount of the payment is calculated by subtracting the amount of income that was paid out from the original premium. After the final payout, the account is closed.

"Ten years certain" is a plan where income is paid for a minimum of 10 years. If the annuity owner dies after receiving only payments for three years, his or her beneficiary receives the income for another seven years. The number of years is written into the contract at the time the annuity is bought. Thus, the purchaser can buy an annuity with an option of 10 years certain, 15 years certain, 25 years certain, or whatever he or she wishes.

Joint annuities work in the same way regarding payments. Assuming a 10 year certain contract, if one of the owners dies after receiving payments for three years, the other owner or beneficiary will receive payments for the remainder of the contract.

134

VARISWISS: THE FIRST SWISS VARIABLE ANNUITY TAILOR-MADE FOR INTERNATIONAL INVESTORS

When going global with part of your assets, the goal should be to optimize profit and achieve long-term security coupled with tax-saving benefits and asset protection possibilities. An investment that offers all this and guarantees liquidity and flexibility at all times is the ideal safe haven investment for your global investment portfolio.

Until recently, variable annuities, also known as "fund-linked insurance policies" or "unit-trust-linked policies," were not available in Switzerland, as they were liable to taxes and therefore not attractive to investors. After a change in Swiss tax law eliminating taxes on variable annuities, the conservative and careful stance of the Swiss insurance industry required an extensive period of review before they decided to include variable annuities in the ranks of solid Swiss insurance products already available to Swiss and foreign investors.

But now variable annuities are available in Swiss francs, historically the world's strongest currency, providing investors with a solid, tax-free financial base. VariSwiss can be self-directed or managed by professional money managers.

VariSwiss Options

There are two VariSwiss options to choose from. VariSwiss 1 is for the internationally aware, more sophisticated investor making his own investment decisions. You make your choice from the 26 available funds according to your own analyses and expectations, buying and selling your fund shares as you desire with the goal of maximizing gains. If you do not wish to choose specific funds immediately, you may initially place your assets in a Swiss franc money market fund and begin to make allocation decisions from there after taking the time to analyze the 26 funds available to you or choosing a specific investment.

135

VariSwiss 2 is for the internationally interested investor eager to profit from global investment opportunities, yet not able or inclined to make specific fund selections on his own. You therefore turn the asset allocation process over to a professional team of money managers at Ticino Life, who have a consulting agreement with UeberseeBank's professional team of international money managers. These two specialized teams analyze world markets and choose specific funds assessed to hold the greatest potential for high yields. Their goal is to maintain a well-balanced portfolio with the opportunity for higher gains.

After you have chosen between VariSwiss 1 or VariSwiss 2, you retain the option to change your choice should you feel at a later date that you would like to become more active in your own decision making, or alternatively, if you would prefer to pass the task of asset allocation on to the management team at Ticino Life. With VariSwiss you can switch to version one or two at any time without incurring any costs or fees.

Should you feel at some time that the world's financial markets are getting too chaotic or hectic and you desire to retreat from any market risk linked investments, VariSwiss gives you the option of switching your variable annuity (which carries a market risk) to a no-risk segregated annuity, which guarantees a base interest plus pays dividend additions (also known as "bonuses" or "profit participation") that provide you with earnings equal to current market interest rates. Your VariSwiss is therefore a true safe haven investment.

VariSwiss Redemption Possibilities

Once you plan to redeem your investment or begin receiving an income, you have the following options:

1) Annuitize VariSwiss in full and receive a regular annual income for as long as you live.

2) Annuitize only a portion of VariSwiss to provide for the life income you require at the time, and the remaining assets continue to accumulate earnings.
3) Liquidate VariSwiss in full, giving instructions where to send the proceeds.
4) Liquidate only a portion of VariSwiss, leaving the remaining assets to continue accumulating earnings.
5) Or if you prefer, you can take physical possession of the fund shares VariSwiss contains.

SWISS ANNUITIES AND THE LEGAL PROTECTION OF ASSETS

Switzerland's long tradition of providing privacy and safety to investors is extended to annuities. This is vital to investors who want to ensure that their growing investments are not subject to claims by individuals or governments.

Swiss law ensures that insurance policies, including annuities, cannot be seized by creditors. Moreover, such policies cannot be included in a Swiss bankruptcy procedure. The investor enjoys protection from foreign governments in the matter of bankruptcy as well. An American court may expressly order the seizure of a Swiss annuity account or its inclusion in a bankruptcy proceeding, but provided that the account has been structured in the proper way, Swiss authorities will not seize it.

Two requirements are essential here. First, a U.S. resident who buys a life insurance policy from a Swiss insurance company must designate his or her spouse or descendants, or a third party if done so irrevocably, as beneficiaries. Second, to avoid suspicion that the policy was bought to circumvent a specific judgment, under Swiss law the investor must have purchased the policy or designated the beneficiaries not less than six months before any bankruptcy decree or collection process.

The following example illustrates how an investor can protect his annuity. Suppose the investor learns that his creditors intend to seize his assets. He assumes that if this happens a court will order him to repatriate the funds in any insurance policy he owns. He immediately designates his wife or children as beneficiaries. He makes sure that this is an irrevocable designation. If he is then ordered by the court to change the designation of the beneficiary and liquidate the annuity, he will not be able to because the beneficiary designation is irrevocable. The insurance company will not accept his changes.

In the case of bankruptcy, the Swiss insurance law Article 81 provides that if the owner of an annuity makes a revocable designation of spouse or children as beneficiaries, they automatically become owners of the annuity and acquire all rights if the original owner declares bankruptcy. If this were to happen, the original owner would have to relinquish control of the policy because the Swiss law turns a revocable designation into an irrevocable designation as a consequence of a bankruptcy filing. He therefore loses his right to liquidate and use the money of the fund for any other purpose, including the repatriation of funds. Even a court cannot force him to do so.

It is vital that a Swiss insurance company be notified promptly of the bankruptcy of an annuity holder so that they can note this in their records. This way, even if a court orders the original policyholder to liquidate the annuity, the insurance company will not act on those instructions.

As long as the owner of an annuity or insurance policy designates his spouse or children as beneficiaries, the policy is protected from creditors. It doesn't matter whether his beneficiaries have been designated as revocable or irrevocable. The policyholder can take advantage of this by designating his spouse or children as beneficiaries on a revocable basis, and then, provided there are no threats from creditors, change that designation before the policy expires.

THE SECURITY PROVIDED BY SWISS LAW

Many offshore islands these days boast of having special laws and regulations that enable investors to create a variety of trusts that supposedly protect the investor's assets. Unfortunately, since such legislation is not part of the actual governing laws of the country but something designed to attract foreign money, it becomes clear that such laws are enacted merely to create a phony trust, the purpose of which is to defraud creditors and ignore true legal title. In fact, most of these trusts are merely used as legal titles to assets that are left in the United States. Since the assets remain in the United States in brokerage accounts or similar institutions, it is relatively simple for American courts to seize them by declaring the so-called offshore trust a sham. In such a case, the foreign law is irrelevant as the U.S. court uses the law of the state in which it is located to determine the issue.

Swiss law governing the financial industry, however, is a part of the country's legal tradition. The laws were not enacted to provide some type of underhanded asset protection but grew out of Switzerland's history and customs. Swiss annuities are not protected by Swiss courts so that investors might use them to ignore creditors, but rather they have been written for the Swiss people.

The Swiss have always supported the idea of wealth building. Annuities are just another means to that end.

MAINTAINING A "BANK ACCOUNT" WITH A SWISS INSURANCE COMPANY

There are many ways to finance the various annuities you may purchase through Swiss insurance companies. Many investors simply make single deposits as necessary, while others decide to use the cost-averaging method.

Although some people make their payments through Swiss bank accounts, this isn't necessary. Many prudent investors feel that paying through a Swiss bank account eliminates one of the major advantages of Swiss insurance and that is privacy. Maintaining a Swiss bank account is reportable under U.S. laws.

A premium deposit account is an alternative. This is an interest bearing bank account that you open at your insurance company. These accounts offer several important and special features. A premium deposit account is not reportable to tax authorities because deposits are made to an insurance company and not a bank. Premium deposit accounts also pay interest rates about a percent higher than the typical savings accounts that banks offer. In addition, you pay no withholding tax on interest, and all payments are tax free.

There are no restrictions on how much you can deposit in a premium deposit account, although the minimum deposit is SFr100. To open the account, just send the funds to your insurance company and instruct them that you want to obtain a premium deposit account. You use your policy number in the same way you would use a bank account number. You will receive an annual statement summarizing your account.

It is advisable, although certainly not required, that you make annual payments from your premium deposit account. Swiss insurance companies make surcharges of 2, 3, and 5 percent for semiannual, quarterly, and monthly premium payments, respectively. By making an annual payment and using your premium deposit account for small deposits throughout the year, you reduce the number of surcharges. You can also save by making deposits when the exchange rate is most favorable.

There are some limitations to premium deposit accounts, however. You cannot purchase gold, securities, or other investment products from a premium deposit account. It can be used only as an interest-bearing Swiss franc account from which you can authorize the making of automatic premium payments. When the premium on an annuity is due, the insurance company merely deducts the payment from your account.

SWISS ANNUITIES AND UNITED STATES TAXES

Tax laws are complex; therefore, careful attention must be paid to details when buying annuities in order to save you money. This is especially true regarding estate tax implications, which greatly depend on which beneficiary option the contract contains.

Taxes on the income payments of an annuity are based on the amount of life income received each year. In calculating tax requirements, the IRS divides the total premium payment by the number of years the annuity owner is expected to live. Those years are based on life expectancy tables for the investor's age at the time he or she is to start receiving payments.

To help clarify some of these points about taxes, let's take an example. Suppose a 65-year-old man, whose life expectancy is an additional 15 years, buys a Swiss annuity worth $10,000. This premium payment divided by 15 years equals $666.67 per year, which is the nontaxable part.

The life income from this annuity is a fixed amount in Swiss francs, but the dollar amount the man receives each year fluctuates. Suppose he receives $850 during the first year. His taxable income then is $183.33 ($850 minus $666.67). If he receives any profits due to currency appreciation, the profits are taxed as ordinary income in the year they are received. If, because of currency depreciation, his income comes out to be less than $666.67, he can claim that as a loss.

In the case of the same 65-year-old man—if he lives beyond his life expectancy of 15 more years, payments received each year after the 15 years are taxed as ordinary income. If, however, he dies before the 15 years are up, the unrecovered part of his premium is deductible on his final income tax return.

The responsibility of reporting earnings on any annuity falls to the investor. The Swiss insurance company makes no reports of purchase, payments, or profits.

Swiss annuities offer investors various options in wealth building. Without doubt there is a Swiss annuity that is right for your financial needs. All that remains is for you to select the one that best meets your financial goals.

UTILIZING THE SERVICES OF A SWISS INVESTMENT CONSULTANT

Although international investors can handle their investments in Switzerland themselves, by far the most practical way to enter the Swiss financial markets and the opportunities they offer is to send a letter to a Swiss insurance broker who specializes in foreign business. He can provide you with all the information you need to make the investment choices that are right for you.

Few transactions can be concluded directly by foreigners either with a Swiss insurance company or with Swiss insurance agents. Legally, they can handle the business, but foreign investors aren't their usual clientele.

I recommended that you contact JML Swiss Investment Counsellors. JML is an independent group of financial advisors. They have a wealth of experience that they can share with their clientele. Since 1974 they have specialized in Swiss franc insurance, gold, and selected Swiss bank-managed investments for European and overseas investors. Currently the group services close to 16,000 clients throughout the world, with investments through JML of more than one billion francs. JML represents SwissPlus and VariSwiss programs that are discussed in this book.

JML charges you no fee because they are paid by the companies with which you invest your money. Their commissions and fees are standard for the financial industry, and all transactions are strictly regulated by the Swiss authorities.

You will find JML easy to work with. Their staff is fluent in English and they understand the special concerns of the international investor. They are knowledgeable and aware of the details that are crucial to you as a foreign investor. They will be able to answer your questions about investments, potential taxes, and legalities. Contact:

JML Jurg M. Lattmann AG
Swiss Investment Counsellors
Baarerstrasse 53, Dept. 212
CH-6304 Zug, Switzerland
Telephone: (41) 42 26 55 00
FAX: (41) 42 26 55 90; Attn: Dept. 212

When you contact JML, be sure to include the following information:

Your name
Address
Telephone number
Date of birth
Marital status
Citizenship
Number of children and their ages
Name of spouse

Also include a clear explanation of your financial objectives and whether the information is for a corporation, individual, or both. You might also wish to include the possible dollar amount that you are interested in investing.

Without question, Swiss banks are among the safest in the world. When you factor in the variety of services they offer, it is easy to see why they are the choice of investors worldwide.

12 The Advanced Strategies that Few Lawyers Know

In this chapter, I illustrate how new and innovative strategies are being created every day to protect assets and create a safe and predictable environment for asset protection consumers. The old days of single shot plans are gone. It is also important to understand that many historically used strategies for income tax mitigation and deferral of taxation are currently integrated into well-thought-out asset protection plans. Several of these strategies are going to be discussed here. All of the new strategies discussed here were created by Asset Protection Corporation, Suite 201A, 14418 Old Mill Road, Upper Marlboro, MD, 20772. Asset Protection Corporation is a management team of lawyers, investment advisors, and accountants that works with lawyers (as well as directly with clients) throughout the country. They will send a free information package on request.

INTERNATIONAL TRUST COMPANIES

It is becoming more and more common for international trust companies to cater to Americans for purposes of offshore investment. The common scenario today is that by using money managers specializing in global investing and a mixture of investment and insurance products, the financial expatriate can find a superior yield in his portfolio with less risk.

More importantly, the flavor of the portfolio can be tailored to the individual's specific estate planning goals, thereby benefiting children, business partners, spouses, and an entire array of other beneficiaries who may in some past scenarios have been treated less than fairly.

The international trust company is a way of providing a menu of investment opportunities to the client. While the trust company combines the proper financial planning with the smorgasbord approaches to investment, each person receives a very high degree of protection and an individually tailored portfolio. Many times the advantage of this approach is lower administrative fees, better recording on an omnibus basis, and a better managed financial and estate plan.

These international financial mechanisms are being set up all the time. One of their important aspects that must be recognized is the ultimate depository of the money involved. It is quite important that the resting place of the capital involved be safe and secure. Examples of this include Swiss banks, English banks, and other institutions of long-standing integrity that can assure the client that they are not in a scam haven.

One of the attractive portions of these offshore arrangements is the use of the estate planning tools that can allow for enhanced estate tax treatment. If done without this overview, many times this portion of the plan fails. Asset Protection Corporation has developed some unique approaches to offshore trusts, including strategies of having the trust company incorporated in one country, the administrative management in a second country, and the actual assets kept in major banks in a third country. This may sound expensive, but it actually costs less than traditional methods, since the best services in the world can be contracted at the best prices instead of trying to do everything in a small tax haven that may not be adequate to the task.

One of the very attractive features of these international trust companies is the use of a variable annuity. A captive insurance company in an offshore environment can create a tax deferred environment within which an investment account can reside. This means that there are no taxes on the money accumulated in this vehicle until the point in time when that money is brought back into the country. This can be a tremendous advantage to the overall growth of this vehicle.

PRIVATIZE YOUR SOCIAL SECURITY

Another strategy that has been used for many years is dividend or profit distribution from "pass-through" entities in order to decrease social security costs. An example of this is as follows: You have a current business that pays fees to a limited liability company or some other pass-through entity (such as a partnership or an S corporation) in return for services that are provided by that pass-through entity. An example of the services provided is management by an owner of this company.

For many years, in properly constructed asset protection plans, I have seen the separation of valuable assets from the corporate entity. This is because over the years many people have accumulated large numbers of assets in their corporations, not realizing that they were in fact creating a target for lawsuits.

It is not uncommon at all for a young entrepreneur to start his corporation to shield his personal assets, yet as the business grows he buys real estate, accumulates accounts receivable (a very common occurrence in medical practices, where the largest single asset is often accounts receivable), as well as patents, licenses, and other valuable assets.

If a limited liability company is added, it can pay

147

income to a family limited partnership created through the estate planning of the principals. As money travels from the corporation, fees are paid to the limited liability company where the consultant takes a salary of some dollar amount, and the rest of the fees are treated as dividends or as a distribution of profits. When this occurs, there is a difference between the income received that is subject to FICA and the total distribution of profits. In other words, to use a rough example, if two-thirds of the distribution of profits is made not subject to FICA, there will be a decrease in the payments for social security.

Always be aware that invoking this strategy will most assuredly result in lowering the social security benefit. Only those persons who are philosophically attuned to this fact will ultimately take responsibility for this action, save that money, invest it prudently, and allow this to serve as their barrier to poverty at retirement age. This is not a program designed to produce money for a vacation to Cancun or a new automobile; this is sacred retirement money and should be treated as such. One of the main elements of this whole plan is clearly the element of self reliance and social responsibility. We don't want a population dependent on the government as we have now. Any citizen who can take personal responsibility for their own financial well-being should be encouraged to do so.

Now, many questions come up as to what to do with the excess. Certainly investment accounts are a logical place for this money to rest. If you are looking for a tax deferred environment, then it is quite obvious that typical tax deferred/asset protection vehicles like insurance and annuities are a perfect choice. With the new products available, including variable life insurance and variable annuities, which allow for the investment into tax deferred vehicles of money, historically going into mutual funds, one can either provide a financial safeguard to a family using life insurance, or one can use an annuity.

In certain cases, there is an ultimate advantage to using the life insurance investment because of the peculiar tax treatment of the life insurance vehicle. Specifically, this is called "washed loan accounting." When a person makes an investment into a life insurance policy and gains are created, the tax deferments build up the gains until retirement, when the person starts to withdraw from the policy.

In these cases, people draw long and expansive income streams because of the tax treatment of the withdrawal. The first monies withdrawn from the policy are considered to be withdrawals and are therefore nontaxable. The rest of the capital gains are taken out of the policy under a "washed loan program," which means that the account is credited the same or a similar interest rate as the loan applied to the withdrawal. The result is a wash loan. The value of a wash loan is that because it is a loan, it is not treated as a taxable event.

There is no reason to believe that wash loans will exist long into the future. Taxpayers should get information on these programs as soon as possible. Because of the many changes made in the tax law, they tend not to be retroactive, but they do tend to be grandfathered. The purchase of such a contract today could be quite advantageous in many ways.

This FICA reduction program is not one that can be done in a cookie cutter fashion. Each case requires separate and distinct analysis from two perspectives. First, there cannot be an unreasonable alteration of the tax positioning. Second, there must be other reasons for this to take place than simply to effect a tax result. There are numerous cases in both of these situations that can give the taxpayer guidance. It is imperative that knowledgeable and experienced legal counsel be at least consulted in constructing such a plan to ensure that the IRS doesn't disallow the program, which would result in back payments having to be made to social security.

149

Very few financial planners are even aware of the possibilities for FICA reduction. For more information and referral to people in your area who can help, write to FICA Reduction Program, P.O. Box 540, Upper Marlboro, MD, 20772.

NO-LOAD INSURANCE

Many investors have become accustomed to no-load mutual funds, which have become attractive for many reasons. These investors have been able to seek out investment opportunities that they could manage themselves. They felt that the commissions they normally paid to brokers were wasted. What the investor may not have done is a complete analysis of what the actual management costs hidden in the no-loads are, and there is considerable debate in the industry as to whether load or no-load funds perform best in the long term.

One of the things that people are tremendously unaware of is the extremely high commission load in insurance products. The reason for this is simple. Insurance is probably the hardest financial vehicle to sell, and it is sold in a much slower period of time from beginning of sale to end than typical investments. There also is almost always a requirement that agents spend considerable time in the education process with the client. The average first year load on a policy is 165 percent, 55 percent going to the agent. Even if the planner's fees were equal to the agent's commission, a superior product would still be provided to the client because the agent generally gets 20 to 30 percent, the expense allowance being 10 to 15 percent for the agent and the fringe benefit costs for agents being 6 to 7 percent plus advertising costs. None of these exist in the no-load companies. What this finally results in is a higher cash value on the permanent product or a lower premium on the term insurance product. A higher cash value is very important because it can significantly shorten the period of time one must pay premiums in order to pay up the contract.

A very untypical but attractive strategy that we see being used today uses second-to-die insurance in concert with a family limited partnership. By the partnership owning the second-to-die policy, it is possible to create a death benefit for the payment of taxes at the death of the second party and yet create the ability for the taxpayer to invade the cash values during the lifetime of the husband or wife for purposes of retirement income. This is an excellent example of first-in-first-out (FIFO) accounting. Cash value builds rapidly in a no-load product and at retirement you start taking cash out on a no tax basis, first from withdrawal, then from this wash loan, and ultimately an amount of money far greater than was contributed to the plan becomes available.

A note to add: you may not draw all the money out of the life insurance policy because if the policy lapses prior to death, a taxable event occurs. So an amount of money must be left in the contract in order to sustain the death benefit. This is advisable for clients who wish to leave a legacy for children, charitable contributions, or for the payment of estate taxes, which as we all know are going to get worse and worse.

As this book goes to print, there is a bill in Congress calling for a reduction in the $600,000 federal estate and gift tax to $200,000, with an increase in the top taxable bracket from 50 percent to 70 percent. This could have a devastating effect on the transfer of wealth in this country and needs to be dealt with by prudent and aggressive planning. No-load insurance is a very valuable alternative to this and perhaps someday will be as common as no-load mutual funds. For many years, the insurance industry has paid their agents handsomely for producing high profit business with absolutely no reservations about the system and agent quality. What has resulted, however, is many cases where the unsophisticated agent

151

has sold large amounts of insurance in return for a huge commission and actually done harm to the taxpayer by not being aware of proper planning. One of the best examples of this is the personal ownership of a life insurance policy that now adds to and exacerbates the federal estate tax problem of the taxpayer.

As people become aware of no-load insurance as an alternative, they will have more reason to integrate insurance into their asset protection, financial, and estate planning. Asset Protection Corporation is so far the only company using no-load insurance in asset protection planning.

In essence, no-load insurance is an insurance contract that comes to you from the insurance company without paying commissions to an agent. By retaining an organization that will help you through the problems, this arrangement gets you high quality planning expertise in addition to a superior insurance product. The retention of an insurance consulting firm is almost always done on an hourly basis, and in many cases the cost of the time required to enlarge the need, shop for the proper carrier, complete the application process, take you through the underwriting, and actually produce an end product that is properly structured with the estate or financial plan is far less than the typical commission. The planning is probably better in those organizations that are adept and experienced in these matters, but there aren't many of them. This is not a common practice because the income derived from this approach is far less than in the previously alluded to scenario.

However, you do want to find an organization that has the following professionals associated with it: attorneys, accountants, charter life underwriters, chartered financial consultants, registered investment advisors, and professionals who are practicing in an area of sophisticated business tax and estate planning that have less vested interest in providing insurance and more in appropriate planning and detailed analysis. Many consumers as well as financial professionals have never heard of no-load insurance.

Are the companies good, and what kind of choices do they give you? Many of the companies that are now offering these no-load products are A+ rated by more than one rating agency. What is also interesting is the wide variety of products that are in the marketplace. A typical provider of this service should be able to give you the names of 10 to 12 different companies, each offering approximately 30 different products. These can include term insurance, whole life insurance, second-to-die insurance, variable universal life, first-to-die, disability and flexible differed annuities. If your advisors haven't heard of this yet, write to No-Load Insurance, P.O. Box 540, Upper Marlboro, MD, 20772 and ask for information and a referral to a professional in your area.

SWISS SECOND-TO-DIE INSURANCE

Another alternative that is presenting itself more and more is Swiss second-to-die life insurance. One of the reasons a person buys such a policy is if they decide to take an offshore position and there really is little or no point in investing large amounts of money in life insurance policies held in the United States. It is true that there are many states that offer exempt asset status to life insurance policies as well as annuities, and this should be factored into the equation. But there also are many states that do not. If you move between states, you may jeopardize your exempt status, and some lawsuits may be decided on laws other than your state's. For example, you live in Florida where insurance is exempt from seizure, but you have an accident in another state where insurance is not exempt. If the insurance company is licensed to do business in both states, and it probably is, then the policy may be seized in the state where the accident occurred.

153

If you wish to take the completely offshore approach to your planning, Swiss second-to-die has some very attractive features. Swiss insurance companies, which are historically much more soundly run than American companies, offer products that are not only quite competitive but have a tremendous possible investment advantage as well. This advantage can best be described as the following: if you buy Swiss insurance, change your dollars into the Swiss franc and make your investments in the Swiss franc. Over the last two decades there has been a tremendous decline in the value of the dollar against the Swiss franc. There is no reason to assume that this won't happen in the future. As this occurs, and as the Swiss franc becomes more and more valuable, it is possible that when this money is brought back into the United States or used for retirement purposes in some other jurisdiction, the increase in value from the dollar to the Swiss franc will produce a profit incentive far above what a person would normally assume that they can get from an insurance policy.

As far as the safety of Swiss insurance companies goes, an interesting kind of analysis takes place. It would make the average Swiss actuary shudder to understand what the reserve requirements are for an American insurance company. The Swiss are historically prone to over reserve everything, and their insurance companies are by far one of the best examples.

It is probable that at some time in the future, American insurance companies will fall victim to the same kind of bad press that the savings and loan institutions did. One of the reasons for this is the high incidence of use of derivatives in insurance company portfolios, especially among the weaker companies. Derivatives already carry a very bad reputation, and one of the problems with this scenario is that even if the derivatives are not responsible for a significant weakening in the portfolio of the insurance company, the mere

154

perception may cause people to withdraw their money, creating illiquidity in the insurance company portfolio for sales of valuable assets and a general loss in the value of these portfolios.

Therefore, if one were absolutely convinced of the cause of this type of regulatory instability existing in the United States and sought a safer and more predicable environment, it would be a very normal course of business to seek a Swiss insurer who is able to provide the financial underpinning for these insurance products that is certainly necessary in today's market.

PROTECTING AN INDIVIDUAL RETIREMENT ACCOUNT

People often place foreign securities, bank certificates of deposit, or Swiss annuities into an Individual Retirement Account. The problem with this strategy is that legally the investments are owned by a United States trustee or custodian within the terms of the retirement account contract. Such accounts are not exempt assets and can be seized in lawsuits, forfeitures, or by the IRS.

A better way is a little-noticed section of the U.S. Internal Revenue Code, which creates a parallel entity to the Individual Retirement Account called the Individual Retirement Annuity. The U.S. Internal Revenue Code requires a United States trustee and a United States custodian for an Individual Retirement Account, but it does not require these for an Individual Retirement Annuity. You can therefore roll over distributions of your entire account from corporate pension and Keogh plans into an offshore Individual Retirement Annuity and thereby acquire a great measure of asset protection.

The IRS does require that the special tax conditions of the retirement annuity be written into the annuity contract, and most foreign insurers are unwilling to modify their standard policies or in many cases are unable to get their local insurance regulators to permit them to modify a policy to include wording required by another government.

The foreign Individual Retirement Annuity is not practical for a small account receiving continuous contributions, but it is a very elegant solution for a person with a large sum to roll over from an existing pension plan, and it is the only way to get a pension plan fully offshore instead of just having an offshore trustee hold a foreign asset. So far only Asset Protection Corporation has been able to negotiate the appropriate policies with foreign insurers, but they will work with financial professionals and attorneys who wish to use the service as well as directly with individual clients.

13 The High Ground of Judgment-Proofing

HONESTY IS THE BEST POLICY

One of the greatest problems of asset protection planning is the naive fool who breaks laws without thinking through the consequences.

So many people think that using secrecy instead of a carefully made plan is the solution to their problem. There is no such thing as a "secret" bank account for an American, because it is a felony to fail to immediately notify the government of the existence of the account. The penalties for such secrecy are far worse than they are for any possible tax offense, and recently the penalties have been increased so severely that no American should even contemplate such a violation. One bribed bank clerk (perhaps for a mere $100) in a so-called secrecy jurisdiction could put the client in prison for 10 to 15 years under new mandatory minimum sentencing laws.

As this book has shown, there are so many legitimate ways that a U.S. citizen can have asset protection without running afoul of these draconian laws that nobody needs to do illegally what they can do legally.

The most dangerous fools—to themselves as well as to everyone they deal with—are those individuals who fail to understand the serious implications of their actions. They deal with lawyers, accountants, and/or bankers as if there was nothing legally wrong with their actions and then seem startled when the family accountant or banker who is facing many years in prison testifies against them because he was dragged into something he had no intention of being a part of. Or worse, they wind up blurting out their incriminating intentions to a lawyer or accountant, who immediately notifies the authorities that are frequently setting a trap for them. (Remember, lawyer-client confidentiality does not apply to stating an intention to commit a crime, and the lawyer is legally obligated to report it.) Many United States professionals today (perhaps fearing a possible setup by authorities) venture on the side of caution and immediately report such approaches. This is no secret—it has been recorded in many court cases—but the naive clients continue to get convicted.

The penalties for most of the bank secrecy and money laundering crimes ("money laundering" includes moving unreported cash, even if you are the legal owner) are several times the penalty for armed bank robbery. Most of these people would never consider committing a bank robbery, and if they were to plan such a crime, they would choose their partners with extreme care and full awareness of the consequences by all parties concerned. Yet they think nothing of committing and cavalierly involving others in financial crimes with far more serious penalties as if it were a big joke and nothing to be seriously concerned about.

GETTING STARTED

This book presents a wide range of possibilities. It is important to remember that it is not necessary to do everything at once. Not only might the degree of protection you need vary, but you may not want to change all of your investment structures immediately, unless, of course, you are facing an immediate problem.

It is perfectly feasible to start out slowly, perhaps by putting your brokerage account into a Delaware limited partnership, later adding a foreign annuity, and still later adding an offshore asset protection trust. Or you may decide that there is no need to go offshore at all and accomplish your goals within domestic structures instead.

Cost is a factor as well. The term "asset protection" was popularized by a few promoters charging very high fees to have their secretaries pull a cookie-cutter offshore trust off their word processors. Those fees are often in the $25,000 to $50,000 range.

Every case is different, but by using the resources in this book, you will be able to create a better strategy for a fraction of the cost. Depending on the complexity of your needs, fees may range from under $5,000 to perhaps $10,000 or $15,000 to set up a comprehensive asset protection plan. Anything more than that should make you nervous. More money does not necessarily mean better quality.

Your profession may dictate your needs—obviously a medical practitioner has more reason for a complex structure than the average person, and a neurosurgeon even more so since his risk of suit is even higher. But a retired gas station owner, who appears at first glance to have little risk, may have a lurking liability problem from the station he sold a decade ago, when some future builder discovers contaminated soil from a leaking gas tank on the site that nobody knew about at the time. His exposure and his total net worth may not justify the expense of an offshore asset protection trust, but he may find a Swiss annuity to be a perfect solution.

You could very easily set up a regular domestic living trust to avoid probate, but in a country where you know people go crazy with lawsuits, why not just take out the extra protection and get an asset protection trust? It is an added benefit for the regular user of trusts. Which brings me back to the point about asset protection not being something that can be done in a vacuum.

Not everybody who insures their home against fire is an arsonist, but people looking for pure lawsuit protection pose difficulties, as do would-be insurees looking to insure against a single risk like fire rather than all the risks to which a property is vulnerable. Likewise, the person engaged in overall financial and estate planning, in which asset protection is just one benefit, is in a different category.

About the Author

Adam Starchild is the author of over a dozen books and hundreds of magazine articles, primarily on business and finance. His articles have appeared in a wide range of publications around the world, including *Business Credit, Euromoney, Finance, The Financial Planner, International Living, Offshore Financial Review, Reason, Tax Planning International, Trusts & Estates*, and many more.